INVESTIGATING HISTORY

ANCIENT GREECE

Peter Kent and Sue Cosson

SIMON & SCHUSTER
EDUCATION

Text © Peter Kent, Sue Cosson and George Middleton
Artwork © Peter Kent

Photocopying
Multiple copies of the pupils' notes may be made
without payment or the need to seek specific permission
only by the purchasing schools for use in teaching in these schools.
In all other cases, permission to photocopy and distribute
photocopies of these materials must be sought.

First published in 1993 in Great Britain by
Simon & Schuster Education
Campus 400, Maylands Avenue
Hemel Hempstead, Herts HP2 7EZ

**A catalogue record for this book is
available from the British Library**

ISBN 0 7501 0393 0

Designed by Helen Castle
Illustrated by Peter Kent
Printed in Great Britain by
Dotesios Ltd, Trowbridge, Wiltshire

Contents

General Introduction 4
Resources 5
Historical Introduction 6
 1 Ancient Greece and Ancient Britain 10
 2 Ancient Greece 12
 3 Athens and Sparta 14
 4 Growing Up 16
 5 Women 18
 6 Slaves 20
 7 A Family House 22
 8 Sea Transport and Trade 24
 9 Farming 26
10 Religion 28
11 Language 30
12 Myths and Legends 32
13 The Theatre 34
14 Sport 36
15 Music 38
16 Architecture 40
17 Sculpture 42
18 Scientists and Philosophers 44
19 The Persian Wars 46
20 Greece and Rome 48
Resource Sheet 1 – Greek Glossary 50
Resource Sheet 2 – The Greek Alphabet 51
Resource Sheet 3 – Greek Architecture 52
Resource Sheet 4 – Famous Greek Buildings 53
Resource Sheet 5 – A Greek Trireme 54
Resource Sheet 6 – Greek Costume 55
Resource Sheet 7 – The Greek World (map) 56

General Introduction

Investigating History is a series of photocopiable resources designed to cover the National Curriculum for History at Key Stage 2. The Programmes of Study are covered through the full range of skills required in the Attainment Targets.

The series offers one book for each History Study Unit. Each book contains a general introduction, an historical introduction, 20 units and a set of Resource sheets. A unit consists of a double-page spread of teacher's notes and a pupils' activity sheet which may be photocopied. Each unit presents stimulating activities which encourage a skills-based investigative approach to History.

Listed below are the Attainment Targets and the outline for the History Core Study Unit 5 – Ancient Greece.

Attainment Targets:
AT1 Knowledge and understanding of history:
   a) change and continuity
   b) causes and consequences
   c) knowing about and understanding different features of past situations.
AT2 Interpretations of history
AT3 The use of historical sources

Core Study Unit 5 Ancient Greece	Units in book
The city state	3, 6
The economy	8, 9
Everyday life	3, 4, 5, 6, 7, 12
Greek religion and thought	10, 18
The arts	10, 12, 13, 15, 16, 17
Relations with other peoples	19, 20
The legacy of Greece	11, 12, 14, 16, 20

Using the book

The following paragraphs give a brief explanation of how the activity sheets and the different sections in the teacher's notes work.

Activity sheets
In general, the activities are suitable for individual, group or class work. The activity sheets are intended to provide stimuli to both teachers and pupils which may then lead to the development of individual or group historical enquiry. The sheets are not intended to be worked through methodically; teachers will wish to select and adapt the activities and ideas to suit the needs of the children.

The resource sheets at the back of the book are intended to supplement particular activity sheets; indication is given in the teacher's notes if and when a resource sheet may be relevant.

Teacher's notes
- The *Skills* section lists the historical skills which the children will be developing in working on the activity sheet.

- The *National Curriculum* charts indicate the Attainment Targets which will be studied through working on the activity sheet and extension activities.

- The *Background information* section gives useful historical information, particularly highlighting some areas with which children and teachers may be unfamiliar.

- The *Introductory work* section gives suggestions for pre-experience and ways of introducing the sheets.

- The *Using the sheet* section details any equipment children might need, explains what the children are expected to do and makes suggestions for prompting questions or activities to help them get the most out of the activity sheet.

- The *Extension activities* often include suggestions for cross-curricular activities and ways of consolidating and extending the skills and knowledge promoted by the activity sheet.

Investigating History should not be seen as the entire scheme of work for a project. Children should also have the opportunity to use a whole range of other resources and, if possible, to visit sites and museums which will further enrich their studies. They should also have access to research and information books which will allow them to investigate particular areas of interest.

Resources

Books for Teachers

In Search of the Trojan War 0 563 20161 4
(*From the BBC series*)
The Ancient Olympic Games (*British Museum*)
0 714 20022
Greek Vases (*British Museum*) 0 714 12030 8
Greek & Roman Life (*British Museum*) 0 714 12041 3
The Elgin Marbles (*British Museum*) 0 714 12026 X
Reading the Past: Greek Inscriptions (*British Museum*)
0 714 18064 5
The Greek Myths (*Robert Graves*) Books 1 & 2
Penguin
The Greeks (*H.D.F. Kitto*) Penguin
A Concise History of Ancient Greece
Thames & Hudson
Classical Greece *Phaidon*
The Aegean Civilisations *Phaidon*
Faber Book of Greek Legends 0 571 13920 5
Women in Ancient Greece and Rome 0 521 31807 6
An Introduction to Greek Mythology 1 850 76169 8
Lion Gate and Labyrinth (*Hans Baumann*) *O.U.P.*
The World of Classical Greece 0 431 96853 6
Greece and the Hellenistic World (*J. Boardman*)
O.U.P.
Atlas of the Greek World *Phaidon*
The Greek World (*R. Ling*) Elsevier-Phaidon

New for the National Curriculum

A Sense of History – Ancient Greece *Longman*
Ancient Civilisations – The Ancient Greeks
Heinemann 0 435 04207 6
Collins Primary History – Ancient Greece
Collins 0 00 315452 3
Themes: The Use of the Classical World in the
National Curriculum for Primary Schools
*Available from: L.B. Forde, St. Mary's College,
Strawberry Hill, Twickenham, Middlesex, TW1 4SX.*

Books for Children

(NB Many of these were written for secondary
schools but often contain useful pictures and extracts
from sources. P indicates that the book will be
accessible to most children in primary schools.)

The Greek Theatre 0 582 34400
Greek Athletics 0 582 20059 8
Greek Everyday Life 0 582 20672 3
The Greek and Roman World 0 631 93330 1
Athletics, Sports and Games 0 049 30006 7
The Ancient World (*pupils' book*) 0 719 53954
(P) The Ancient Greeks Activity Book (*British Museum*) 0 714 11283 6
(P) Minos and the Cretans 0 850 78763
(P) See Inside an Ancient Greek Town 0 862 72204
(P) The Greeks 0 333 49266 8
(P) What do we know about the Greeks?
Simon & Schuster 0 7500 1049 5
(P) A Greek Temple *Simon & Schuster* 0 7500 1081 9
(P) Athens and Sparta *Simon & Schuster*
0 7500 1102 5
(P) Greeks pop-up book 0 906 21233 2
(P) Ancient Greeks 0 435 04207 6
(P) British Museum Paper Pageants 0 224 02380 2
(P) Greek Food and Drink 0 850 78941 9
(P) The World of Ulysses 0 563 34415 6
(P) The Legend of Odysseus 0 199 17065 7
(P) Everyday Life of a Greek Potter *Macdonald*
(P) In Search of Troy 0 356 11254 9
The Iliad 0 192 74147 0
The Odyssey 0 192 74146 2
Heroes and Monsters of Ancient Greece
0 330 29707 4
Greek Myths and Legends 0 860 20946 6
Perseus, the Gorgon Slayer 0 947 21270 1
Jason and the Golden Fleece 0 233 98325 2
The Fables of Aesop 0 856 54060 9
Tales of the Greek Heroes 0 140 35099 3
The Luck of Troy *Puffin*
The Tale of Troy 0 140 35102 7
(P) Monsters of Mythology Series *Chelsea House*
(P) Famous Legends (Books 1 & 2) *Ladybird*
(P) A Second Book of Aesop's Fables *Ladybird*

Audio-Visual

BBC Zig Zag: a useful addition to other resources.
Notes have some good ideas for activities.
British Museum Education Service video loans,
'Childhood in the Greek and Roman World' and
'A visit to the Ancient Olympic Games'.
'Odysseus: The Greatest Hero of them All'
The story of Odysseus as he might have seen it (with
sound effects) on 2 cassettes. *Available from Chivers
Audio Books, Windsor Bridge Road, Bath, BA2 3AX*

Places to Visit

British Museum, London
Fitzwilliam Museum, Cambridge
Museum of Classical Archaeology, Cambridge

Historical Introduction

The civilisations of Egypt, Mesopotamia and Crete were already well advanced when the first Greek-speaking peoples migrated into what is now Greece in about 2000 BC. Gradually a number of small kingdoms emerged, each centred on a strongly fortified royal citadel. The chief of these was at Mycenae and gave its name to this whole early period. The Myceneans learned seamanship and conquered Crete in about 1400 BC after the Minoan civilisation collapsed, probably in a natural disaster. For the next 200 years, the Myceneans dominated the Aegean and eastern Mediterranean.

In about 1100 BC there was a fresh migration into Greece of another Greek-speaking people, the Dorians. Mycenean civilisation collapsed in its turn and Greece reverted to a period of poverty and obscurity about which virtually nothing is known. All the achievements of Mycenae were undone and even the art of writing was lost. Slowly, however, a new society began to emerge. The small dark-age communities evolved into city-states. The Greeks called such a state a *polis* – a small urban centre controlling a surrounding area of arable land. The formation of such unusually small states was a product of geography; the mountainous and broken country made communications difficult and provided each state with formidable natural obstacles for its defence. At first, these states were ruled by kings, but by 800 BC most had passed into the control of aristocracies (the word in Greek means 'government by the best people').

A revival of contacts with the outside world and a growing population prompted trading links and the foundation of colonies along the shores of neighbouring Asia Minor. About this time the Greeks adopted and adapted the Phoenician alphabet. This was of incalculable importance, for it gave them a means to achieve the cultural unity that was such a powerful substitute for political hegemony.

From about 650 BC most of the Greek cities fell under the rule of dictators to whom the Greeks gave the name tyrants. They were largely popular and successful, for the ordinary people were glad to be rid of the aristocracies who had not only denied political rights to the growing numbers of rich merchants and traders, but also pursued economic policies that had increasingly impoverished the peasants. The tyrants diminished the power of the nobles and largely abolished class and racial distinctions, which greatly assisted the rise of democracies two centuries later.

Athens, already by 600 BC one of the most important states, was ruled by a succession of tyrants until a democratic constitution was introduced after a period of civil war in 508 BC. Ironically Greek 'democracy' was only possible because of the spread of slavery, an ample supply of slaves to do the more menial jobs giving the citizens time to attend to the demands of politics. Even though the city-states were small, this system of politics would have been impossibly cumbersome if everyone had taken part. From this democracy, however, women, slaves, and foreigners were excluded.

The sovereign power in Athens was the assembly (*ecclisia*) which consisted of all the adult male citizens. This met every ten days or so on a hill in Athens called the Pnyx – there was no building large enough. A quorum was 6000, contrasting with the 40 needed now for the House of Commons. Every day a new chairman was chosen to preside over the council.

The legal system operated on the same democratic principles. There were no professional judges or lawyers; jurors and the judge were chosen by lot. Even the army command depended on election.

Most of the other city-states had constitutions on similar lines to Athens. The one glaring exception was Sparta. Sparta was unique in the Greek world, a state dedicated solely to military efficiency in which every citizen was a soldier and spent his whole life under rigid discipline. The new-born Spartan was inspected and if pronounced fit allowed to live. At seven he went to what could only be described as a military boarding school. There he lived a rigorous and austere life, with everything devoted to toughening his spirit and his skin. At 20 he joined the army and lived in barracks. At 30 he was allowed to marry and was given land but still spent most of his time in barracks.

This dedication to the military life was only possible because all the work was done by slaves, the helots. As there were far more of them than their masters, the Spartans developed a ruthlessly efficient system of control. The Spartan army was in constant readiness to crush any revolt and controlled the helots with a secret police force which rivalled in brutal efficiency any seen in the twentieth century.

The Spartans made little contribution to the finer aspects of Greek civilisation. They rejected all the arts but music, marching in step to the sound of flutes, and were famed for their brief dour speech (our world laconic comes from Laconia, the region of Greece in which Sparta lies). Even their coinage was nothing more than dull pieces of iron contrasting with the decorative silver coins in use in Athens.

It is important to realise how small these Greek states were. The optimum number of adult citizens was that which could conveniently attend a meeting and make their voices heard. Plato fixed his ideal state at 5040 adult citizens but most Greek states did not even approach that. Mycenae, one of the smallest, had about 600 citizens in 479 BC. Athens, the largest, had about 40,000 citizens, although many of these lived in the surrounding countryside. This made it unusual and of the cities it was probably the

Historical Introduction

most impersonal. Most of the cities were very tightly knit communities, largely related by blood.

Because they were fiercely independent states, warfare between the cities was common for hundreds of years. Every year there was some outbreak of hostilities, although this was not normally serious, consisting of one side invading the other's territory and ravaging the crops. If there was a battle it was short and not particularly bloody. Greek armies – with the exception of the Spartans – were during this period essentially amateur, the citizen soldiers providing their own armour and electing their officers, and they were incapable of prolonged campaigns because of the need to attend to their businesses. All Greek cities were fortified and as the Greek armies had no artillery or siege machines an attack was rarely successful. In normal circumstances it was only treachery or starvation that defeated a city.

In the fifth century BC the Greeks faced their most serious threat: the expanding Persian Empire. The Greek colonies in Ionia in Asia Minor had fallen to the Persians in 546 BC, but they became discontented with Persian rule and revolted in 500 BC. Athens sent help but could not prevent the revolt being suppressed – and this provoked the Persians into forming a plan to send a punitive expedition to mainland Greece.

In 490 BC the Persian king Darius sent a large army to crush Athens. The Persians landed about 30 miles from Athens with about 60,000 men and camped on the plain of Marathon. There they were routed by the Athenians and a small contingent from Platea. Darius died shortly afterwards and it was not for another ten years that a second Persian invasion was attempted by his successor Xerxes.

This time, in 480 BC, the whole might of the Persian Empire was directed to the renewed task of subduing Greece. A vast army and fleet was assembled, composed of elements from throughout the empire, including Greek mercenaries. Legend puts the number of this swarming host at 1,750,000 men, and states that it took seven days to pass over the pontoon bridge that spanned the Hellespont. In reality Xerxes' army was probably no more than 200,000, although this still outnumbered the combined forces of all the Greek cities. But the Greek cities did not combine. Many, terrified by the inexorable advance of the enemy, sent word to Xerxes saying that they would not oppose him and the Persian army marched without much hindrance into Greece. They were checked at the narrow pass of Thermopylae by a force of 300 Spartans, led by Leonidas. All the Spartans were killed before Xerxes' army advanced on Athens.

That Athens and Greece survived is largely due to the foresight of Themistocles, who persuaded his fellow Athenians to spend most of a newly discovered deposit of silver on building a strong fleet. When the Persians advanced Athens was evacuated and the rest of the Greek forces withdrew behind a wall across the isthmus of Corinth. Athens was burnt by the Persians, but the Persians' fleet was destroyed by the Greek navy in a decisive battle at Salamis. Xerxes withdrew, leaving a large force which the combined Greeks, led by Athens and Sparta, defeated at the battle of Platea the next year. These two battles removed the immediate threat of invasion but to counter any future aggression the Greeks formed a defensive alliance called the Delian League. This took its name from the island of Delos where it first met and where the common treasury was held. This classical equivalent of NATO fought the Persians spasmodically for the next 30 years until a peace treaty was signed in 449 BC.

The half century after the defeat of the Persian invasion was the zenith of classical Greek civilisation. The arts of sculpture, architecture and literature all reached extraordinary heights, and the supreme cultural achievement of the age was the rebuilding of the Acropolis of Athens. Under the leadership of Pericles, huge sums were devoted to erecting a complex of buildings that tangibly expressed the glory of Athens and the ideals on which its superiority rested. The Parthenon, designed by Ictinus and adorned with sculptures by Pheidias, is regarded by many as the most perfect building in the world. Its austere elegance conceals a sophisticated manipulation of proportion and mass.

During the middle of the fifth century BC Athens was the major power in Greece. With the largest population and extensive overseas trade and possessions, it was rich, strong and culturally pre-eminent with pretensions to be the leader of the Greek states. Gradually Athens' predominance came to be seen as oppression and resentment grew.

The natural leader of those opposed to Athens was Sparta, which had its own system of alliances and dependent states, in the Peloponnesian League. The more powerful and wealthy the Athenians became, the more the Spartans felt threatened. Fighting broke out in 448 BC but ended the following year. This was the start of the Peloponnesian Wars, however, which after nearly 30 years of fighting were to break the power of Athens and mortally weaken Greece.

In 431 BC the war began in earnest. The ostensible cause was a dispute between Corinth and its colony of Corcyra (modern Corfu). The Athenians backed Corcyra, the Spartans supported Corinth and soon the original quarrel was subsumed within a greater struggle. The Spartans with their powerful army easily invaded Athenian territory, but the Athenians used their powerful navy to harry the Spartans. The war quickly degenerated into a tedious stalemate. Athens, connected by long walls to its port at Pireaus,

Historical Introduction

could not be taken by the Spartans but the Athenians could not prevent the devastation of much of the countryside. The peasants flocked to the protection of the city fortifications and the resulting overcrowding and squalor brought plague which eventually killed a quarter of the population.

Mutual exhaustion resulted in a peace treaty in 421 BC, but war broke out again in 416 BC. The Athenians staked all on an expedition to Sicily to capture the city of Syracuse, which failed.

This disaster caused consternation in Athens and in 411 BC a coup by 400 leading citizens overthrew democracy and established an oligarchy. Defeat followed defeat and many members withdrew from the Delian League. The Persians, seeking to exploit Greek weaknesses, sent subsidies to the Spartans and attacked Athens' allies in Ionia. The Persian money enabled the Spartans to build and equip a fleet, giving them the ability to wage war against Athens at sea as well as on land. In 405 BC the Athenian fleet was destroyed by the Spartans, but not so much through Spartan skill as by the negligence of the Athenian commanders. One hundred and seventy ships and four thousand men were lost. This was the end of Athens. Unable to import corn, it could not hold out against the Spartans and finally surrendered in 404 BC. The long walls connecting Athens to Pireaus were destroyed to the piping of Spartan flutes. The Delian League was dissolved and the power of Athens ended. The Persian Empire gained control of the Greek cities in Ionia and received tribute from Athens as a subject state.

After a brief respite fighting broke out between the Greek cities in 395 BC. The Persians now supported Athens, Thebes, Corinth and Argos against Sparta. Sporadic fighting and shifting alliances continued for the next 20 years until the Thebans gained an unprecedented victory over the Spartans in open battle. With the power of Sparta broken, Thebes was now seen as the major threat to the independence of the Greek states, an independence which they guarded with manic jealousy. Sparta and Athens then made common cause against the Thebans.

While these suicidal struggles were taking place a new power was arising in the north. Macedonia under the leadership of its powerful and acquisitive king, Philip (himself educated in Athens), had been transformed from a poor and semi-barbaric country into a formidably efficient military power. Too late the Greek cities united under the leadership of Athens to meet the Macedonian threat, but they were defeated and marshalled into the Corinthian League under Philip's direction.

The Greeks submitted to this grudgingly, for they regarded the Macedonians as uncivilised, speaking a clumsy dialect and drinking copious amounts of wine unmixed with water. Athenians considered the Macedonian artistic and intellectual achievements negligible. With the Greeks under his control, Philip began to plan a war against Persia, ostensibly as punishment for the sacrilege committed by the burning of the temples on the Acropolis in 480 BC, but also to ensure Macedonia's position as the dominant power in the eastern Mediterranean. But before he could begin the expedition Philip was murdered and succeeded by his twenty-two-year-old son Alexander.

In 334 BC Alexander led 40,000 men across the Hellespont into Asia Minor. Seven years later he stood by the River Indus in what is now Pakistan after conquering the whole of the Persian Empire including Egypt. It was the most extraordinary feat of arms and would have been even more so had his army not mutinied and refused to follow him further into India. Alexander founded cities throughout his conquered territory, naming some after himself and one after his horse. Greek culture, language and beliefs spread throughout the east. (Excavations have revealed a *gymnasium* at Al Khanoum in Afghanistan, as remote a corner of the Hellenistic world as it is possible to find.) Alexander died at Babylon in 323 BC and after a period of struggle the control of his vast empire passed to the descendants of his generals. It was divided into three kingdoms.

During the first eighty years of the third century BC Greek civilisation spread throughout the known world. However, the political and military power of the Greeks began to decline under the combined pressure from east and west.

The Romans conquered the Greek colonies in southern Italy in 275 BC, taking Sicily 60 years later. They then turned east and after a series of wars Macedonia was finally beaten in 146 BC. Greece then became a Roman province although the individual cities maintained a good deal of autonomy and Athens kept its cultural pre-eminence.

Although this was the end of Greek political independence, the influence of Greece was stronger than ever in the Roman Empire. The Romans adopted wholesale the Greeks' art, science and philosophy, rejecting only Greek democracy. As the Roman legions marched into the west they took Greek civilisation with them. In the words of the poet Horace, 'Greece though conquered took her fierce conqueror captive, and brought in the arts to the uncivilised Latin peoples'; through them Greek civilisation was taken to the Celts and the Gauls.

Such was Roman superiority in military and organisational skills that they maintained this civilisation in the west until AD 500 and in Byzantium, in the east, until the fifteenth century. By this time the former barbarians of the west were rediscovering the heritage of Ancient Greek literature, philosophy, art and ideas.

1 Ancient Greece and Ancient Britain Teacher's notes

Skills

Identifying similarities and differences
Making deductions

Attainment Targets

Level	AT1a	AT1b	AT1c	AT2	AT3
1					✓
2		✓		✓	
3		✓		✓	
4		✓			
5					

Background information

Although the Greeks thought of non Greek-speaking people like the tribes of Britain as barbarians, Celtic society seems to have been fairly well organised and prosperous by 500 BC. No doubt there was conflict and rivalry between different tribes, just as there was between Greek city-states. Clearly there are many differences that can be elicited, but it is also worth looking for similarities in order to avoid reinforcing stereotypical views of Ancient Greece and Ancient Britain.

Introductory work

A good starting point would be to ask the children to make a list of the things they would notice about any new place they might visit.
    Children could discuss the problems of showing in one small picture a total view of a society. This could also be done in relation to 20th century Britain.
    What would they include? Different groups might come up with different answers.

Using the sheet

The sheet contains composite drawings of aspects of life in Athens and Celtic Britain. The artist has filled the scene with reconstructed details from a variety of excavations and sites, both from this time and earlier, so that children are able to gain an overview. Points that could be compared include houses, religious buildings, transport, clothing, pottery, weapons, defences, and agriculture. Some of these subjects could be mentioned in the suggested letter home. An alternative method of preparation might be to ask children to produce a chart comparing like with like.

Extension activities

1 Children could investigate one aspect in more detail, using reference books.
2 Groups could discuss what is meant by 'civilised'. This would probably best be done by providing lists of statements about a community from which the children could select those which seem to them to apply to a civilised society, e.g. has a written language, erects religious buildings, has skilled craftsmen etc. Children could decide whether these statements were true of Britain and Greece, perhaps leading to the conclusion that both societies were civilised in their own way. The children could then discuss why the Greeks regarded other societies as barbarians.
3 Children could discuss how a modern artist knows what to put in pictures of the past. This picture in particular could lead to a lot of discussion about the type of evidence which survives from the past.

Ancient Greece and Ancient Britain

The great civilisation of Ancient Greece began to develop over three thousand years ago. We can still see the remains of some of their cities and buildings today. Their ideas, writings and myths spread over a large area, and still influence our world. The Greeks called anyone not part of their Greek-speaking civilisation "barbarians".

2000	1000		0	1000	2000
	BC			AD	

500 BC

Brigantis from Britain and Stratos from Greece are visiting each other's countries in 500 BC. Write a letter home from each listing all the differences between the two places.

© Peter Kent, Sue Cosson and George Middleton. Simon & Schuster Ltd 1993.

2 Ancient Greece

Teacher's notes

Skills
Researching and communicating information
Using a source to stimulate questions about the past
Making deductions from a source

Attainment targets

Level	AT1a	AT1b	AT1c	AT2	AT3
1					√
2					√
3	√				√
4					
5					

Background information

The 'Golden Age' of Classical Greece was from c. 500–c. 300 BC. This is the period of the Persian Wars, of Athenian democracy and of the conflicts with Sparta. Many of the places we associate with Ancient Greece, however, predate the classical period.

The stories of Mycenae, Tiryns and Troy belong to a bronze age civilisation which began about 1600 BC and had collapsed by c. 1000 BC.

Introductory work

It would be useful to start with a 'brainstorming' session to find out what the children know about Greece, ancient or modern. It is possible that it is known mainly as a holiday destination, and the reasons for people choosing to go to Greece today could be discussed. Holiday brochures could be studied to find out what attractions are featured apart from sun and sea and a list of 'historical' places made. This is also a good opportunity of identifying modern Greece on a globe or map, and for finding out information about landscape, climate, main towns etc.

Using the sheet

Quite a lot of discussion will be needed before children can complete the task. Individuals or groups of children could investigate one or more places to find out why it is famous. Then children can write their adverts and decide on places to visit. The sites show: Pella (birthplace of Alexander the Great), Mount Olympus (home of the gods), Troy (10 year war), Thermopylae (300 Spartans fought against Persians), Laurium (silver mines), Athens (Parthenon), Salamis (sea battle with Persians), Corinth (famous for pots), Epidaurus (famous for healing and plays), Olympia (Olympic Games), Mycenae (Lion Gate and citadel), Sparta (Ancient Greece's strongest army), Ithaca (home of Odysseus), Kos (birthplace of Hippocrates), Knossos (Minotaur and labyrinth), Rhodes (Colossus).

Extension activities

1. Children could investigate both the story and the archaeological evidence connected with one of the sites (e.g. the Minotaur).
2. Events connected with the places could be put onto a class time-line. This would show the long period of time spanned and can be added to as the children find out more about Ancient Greece.
3. This would be a good point for the children to list the questions that they would like answered about the Greeks.
4. Like any historical source, three questions can be asked of the map:
   What does it tell us for certain about Ancient Greece?
   What does it suggest about Ancient Greece?
   What questions does it raise?

Ancient Greece

This is a map of Ancient Greece showing the most well known places in the history and legends of the Greeks.

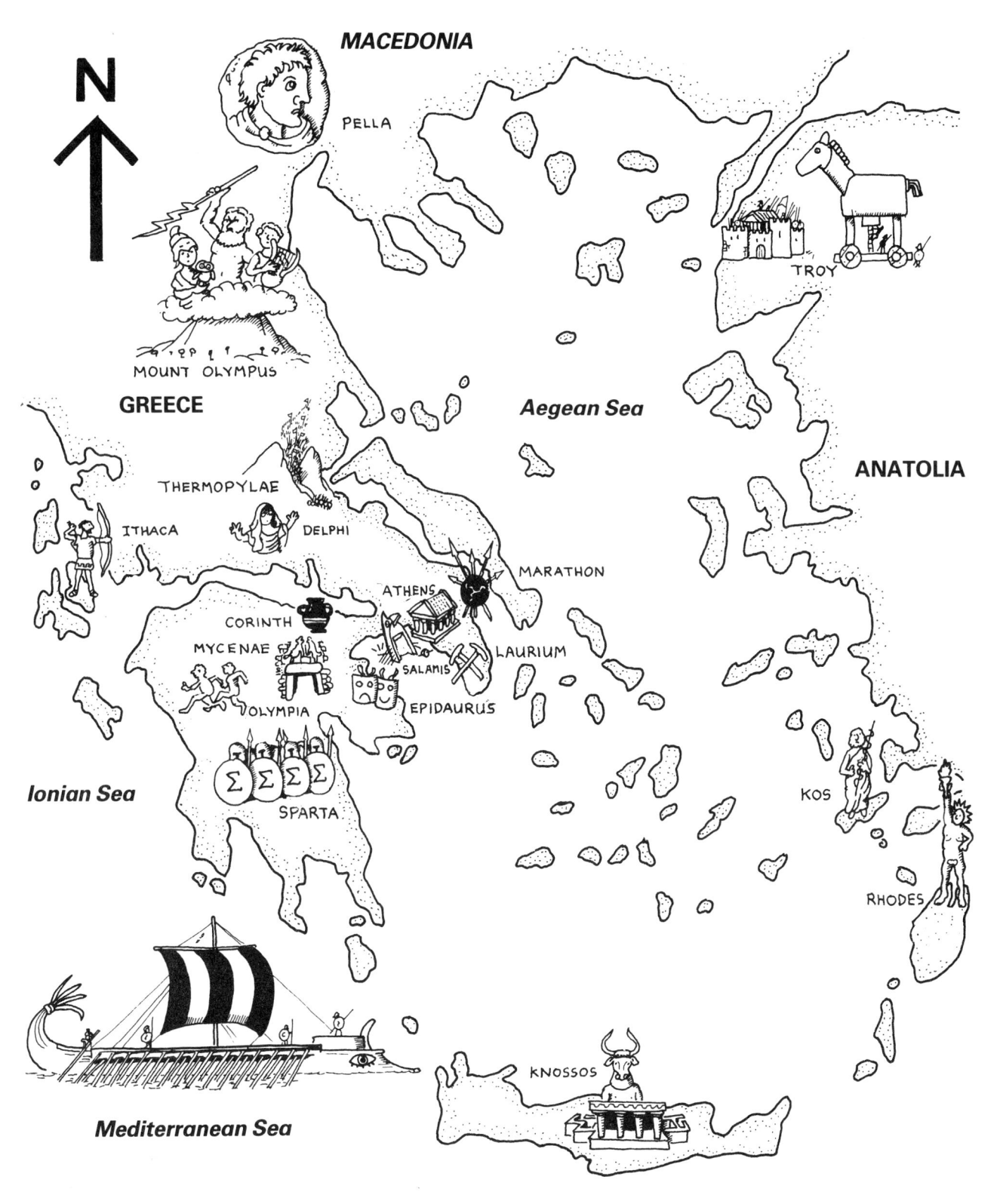

Work out what legend or piece of history each drawing shows. Then write a travel agent's advertisement for a tour of Ancient Greece, listing all the sights and historic monuments.

© Peter Kent, Sue Cosson and George Middleton. Simon & Schuster Ltd 1993.

3 Athens and Sparta

Teacher's notes

Skills

Developing an awareness of the different features of an historical period and how they relate to each other
Understanding the difference between a fact and a point of view

Attainment targets

Level	AT1a	AT1b	AT1c	AT2	AT3
1					
2			✓		
3			✓	✓	✓
4			✓		
5			✓		

Background information

Whereas Athens is famous for its fine buildings, its philosophers, artists and contribution to democracy, Sparta is chiefly remembered for its austere life-style. No fine Spartan ruins are left for us to marvel at, but rather stories of courage, privation and a single minded devotion to the Spartan state.

Introductory work

It might be useful to look up the word 'Spartan' and discuss its meaning, and to retell the story of the Spartan Boy. What does it tell us about the Spartans?

Using the sheet

The sheet focusses on the main differences between Athens and Sparta.
There is a lot of discussion work to be done before children do the activity. Children could be given a contrasting pair of details (e.g. buildings) and asked to deduce what they reveal about Athenian and Spartan attitudes. Their deductions could then be fed into a class discussion about the things that Athenians and Spartans felt to be important. It would be useful to discuss both good and bad points of each of the different aspects, before asking children to make up their mind about where they would prefer to live.

Extension activities

1. Children might research in detail how Spartan children were brought up and compare with their own life. This could be done in the form of time-lines.
2. Children could be asked to carry out further research and produce pictures and captions for a display called 'Sparta, City of Soldiers' or 'Athens, City of Artists and Traders'.
3. Make a series of cards which express opinions that Athenians and Spartans would probably have held (about 10 for each)
   e.g. It's a waste of money to pay for statues
   It's good to be surrounded by beautiful things
   A girl should spend her time at home, learning how to run a household
   It's a good thing for girls to be trained to be fit and healthy.
   Ask children to form groups of Athenians or Spartans and give each group an identical set of cards. Ask them as a group, in role, to decide on 6–8 statements they all agree with. They should find this very easy.
   Now mix up the groups, with some Athenians and some Spartans and, still in role, ask them to pick out 6–8 statements they all agree with. They should find this extremely difficult.
   Discussion should then focus on why it was so difficult to agree the second time and whether the given statements are facts or opinions.

Athens and Sparta

In Ancient Greece every *polis* or 'city-state' was an independent country ruling itself. Some were tiny with only a few hundred inhabitants. The two most important in the 5th century BC were Athens and Sparta. They were very different from one another. Look at the list below to see how.

ATHENS

In Athens the male citizens were soldiers only in time of war

Athens had a powerful fleet

In Athens slaves did much of the work

Athenian girls learnt domestic duties at home

Athens built beautiful buildings

Athens was famous for its learning and culture

Athens traded with different countries and had many foreigners living there

Athens was governed by a form of democracy. Free male citizens made the decisions in the Assembly and elected the officials

SPARTA

In Sparta *all* the male citizens were soldiers *all* the time

Sparta had few ships

In Sparta slaves (*helots*) did *all* the work

Spartan girls played sports and did gymnastics

Spartan buildings were very plain and simple

Sparta had very little art except music

The Spartans kept all foreigners and foreign goods out

Sparta was governed by two kings, five *Ephors* and an assembly of men over sixty

In which of these two cities would you prefer to live? Give your reasons. Could anything change your mind?

© Peter Kent, Sue Cosson and George Middleton. Simon & Schuster Ltd 1993.

4 Growing Up

Teacher's notes

Skills

Sequencing
Using pictorial sources
Recording in visual form

Attainment targets

Level	AT1a	AT1b	AT1c	AT2	AT3
1	✓				✓
2			✓		✓
3					✓
4					✓
5					

Background information

Greek boys received formal education in basic literacy, and in poetry, music and gymnastics. The Greeks loved to talk and listen – they did not lay nearly so much stress on the written word as we do.

The education of girls took place at home, and would include all the business of running a household and bringing up children. Some girls learnt to read and write at home, and they might well be included in the family discussions of politics and current affairs. When a girl married she was carried from her parents' home in a bier, to symbolise the 'death' of childhood and the beginning of her new life.

Introductory work

Children today take it for granted that boys and girls are educated at the same place and in the same way. They may be surprised to learn how recent a development this is, and a class discussion could highlight some reasons for an Ancient Greek system of education, emphasising the types of citizens it was designed to produce. The children could then 'brainstorm' questions they would like answered about growing up in Ancient Greece.

Using the sheet

It would be useful to start by studying the pictures on the sheet and seeing whether any of them answer the above questions. The basic activity is then to cut up a photocopy of the sheet and place the pictures in sequence, from the earliest stage in the boy or girl's life to the latest, providing a written caption to each one. Further research in books will provide more details.

Extension activities

1. The children could be asked to compare the education set out here with their own school experiences, and to suggest modern equivalents of the activities shown – for example, perhaps playing on bikes has replaced the chariot game?
2. The teacher could set up an 'Ancient Greek School Day', with the boys studying writing, poetry and PE, and the girls studying weaving and cookery. (Teachers will have to decide whether the two groups should then try each other's activities!)
3. Working in groups, the children could produce charts based on two columns, one showing what a girl would do during the course of a day, and the other what a boy would do. Illustrations should be based, as far as possible, on original sources from vase-painting etc.
4. Greek children learned to write on wax-covered boards, scratching the letters into the surface with a stylus. The stylus had a flat end which could be used to erase mistakes. Children could experiment with clay or plasticene spread thinly on cardboard, using a pottery modelling tool as a stylus.

Growing Up

Boys had a much more active life than girls, even in Sparta. Girls were educated at home until they got married at about fifteen. Below are fragments of evidence about the lives of Greek children.

A

B

C

D

E

F

G

Put them in the right order of a boy or girl's life and explain what is happening in each picture.

© Peter Kent, Sue Cosson and George Middleton. Simon & Schuster Ltd 1993.

5 Women

Teacher's notes

Skills

Using sources to gain information
Developing an understanding of different points of view
Putting together evidence from more than one source

Attainment targets

Level	AT1a	AT1b	AT1c	AT2	AT3
1					
2				✓	✓
3				✓	✓
4				✓	✓
5					

Background information

Although many traditional textbooks give the view that Greek women were almost totally confined to the home and had no role in the wider community, it should be remembered that much of the surviving evidence was written by men and probably represents society as they wished to see it. Undoubtedly, women played no part in politics, but there is evidence that they undertook a range of economic and religious activities. Women could, for instance, be shopkeepers, physicians, nurses and midwives, musicians and priestesses.

Introductory work

As the focus here is on developing an understanding that there are different versions of the past, it would be a good idea to tackle this idea in a context that is familiar to the children. Some approaches are:
a) to arrange for a colleague to come into a lesson unexpectedly and stage a dramatic incident or deliver a dramatic message. The children can afterwards be asked for their accounts of what happened and reasons for the different versions be discussed. It might also be useful to discuss the difference between fact and opinion
b) to read a traditional fairy story with the children and one of the modern alternative versions offering a different point of view. Children can then discuss how the various characters would view the incidents.

Using the sheet

The sheet can be used quite straightforwardly to identify the pieces of evidence which support the different viewpoints.
An alternative approach would be to photocopy and cut up the sheet and separate the evidence into two groups, A (sources that show women in a purely domestic role) and B (sources that show them in a range of social, economic and religious activities). Children work in pairs and each pair is given set A or set B and the same question, 'What do these sources tell you about what life was like for women in Ancient Greece?' The children are unaware that they have different sources and very different answers to the question will emerge. Having discussed within their pairs, children either report back to the whole class, or the pairs can be mixed up to share what they have found out. It is important that the reasons for conflicting conclusions should be discussed. Try to avoid the question 'Who was right?' but help pupils to see that everybody was right (and everybody was wrong).

Extension activities

1. Give a list of statements about women in Greece to the children, some of which are fact and some opinion. Ask them to sort them into the correct category, e.g. Melitta was an Ancient Greek nurse, Melitta enjoyed being a nurse.
2. Children could be asked to use a range of reference books to find all representations of women in Greek art (i.e. vase paintings, sculptures). They can then identify the activity that is shown and produce a wall display about women in Ancient Greece.

Women

The head of a Greek family was always a man. Women were not allowed to play a part in the world outside the home. They could not vote or fight, for example. They stayed at home doing all the jobs in the house or supervising their slaves. The only important job a woman could do was to be a priestess.

A THIS IS THE TOMB OF HELEN, THE GROCER WHOSE SHOP IS NEAR THE SPRING.

B THIS IS THE TOMB OF MELITTA, A NURSE.

C "The wife is never present at dinner, unless it is in a family party. She spends all her time in the women's quarters which are never entered by a man unless he is a very close relative."

Cornelius Nepus (A Roman)

Nonsense! Greek women were much more involved in life outside the home. Many had jobs and earned their own living.

D SLAVE GIRL

E

F

G "Go to your quarters now and attend to your work, the loom and the spindle ... talking must be the man's concern ... for I am master in this house."

Odysseus, The Odyssey, (Homer)

H

Look carefully at these pieces of evidence. Which seem to support Professor Pick, and which Doctor Shovel?

© Peter Kent, Sue Cosson and George Middleton. Simon & Schuster Ltd 1993.

6 Slaves

Teacher's notes

Skills

Considering motivation of people in the past
Understanding that things happen for a variety of reasons
Rank ordering against predetermined criteria

Attainment targets

Level	AT1a	AT1b	AT1c	AT2	AT3
1					
2		√		√	
3		√			
4		√			
5					

Background information

Slaves were common in all Greek city-states. In Athens the state owned slaves who worked in the silver mines and were not treated well. However, slaves owned by individuals were often treated much better, especially if they were skilled and therefore expensive. Some slaves gained their freedom (often bought with their savings) and set themselves up in business. The Spartans relied on slaves (called 'helots') to do all manual work and the evidence shows they were treated badly. There were constant fears in Sparta of uprisings by the helots.

Introductory work

As an introductory activity, it might be useful to spend some time discussing what it meant to be a slave rather than a servant.
　A good place to start would be discussing what rights children have in school and what they can do if these rights are contravened. They can go on to talk about what it would be like to have no rights, how they might feel if they belonged to someone else and could be bought and sold like an animal. Would it make a difference if the slave was well or badly treated?

Using the sheet

The slaves pictured show a whole range of occupations, some of which would be more valued than others. Children could work in groups to arrange the slaves in order of value after discussing what criteria a slave dealer would use when deciding on a price, e.g. skills, age, health, supply and demand. They will need to think about what the dealer will emphasise when selling each slave (and perhaps try to conceal). The pictures could be cut out individually and mounted with the description and put together as a catalogue for an auction.

Extension activities

1　Children could work in groups to give each of these slaves a background and to decide what thoughts each of them might have as they waited to be sold. They could then act a scene with the 'slave-dealer' trying to convince potential buyers who perhaps talk to the slaves about their skills and experience.
2　Children could research background details to produce a story or strip cartoon of what happened to one of the slaves after being sold. The experiences of the different slaves could be compared, to show reasons why some slaves were more unhappy with their lot than others.
3　Children could research slavery in different societies throughout history, including the present day and produce a time-line. They could research the lives of some of the people who have fought against it e.g. Harriet Tubman, Thomas Clarkson, Alexander Ross, and discuss why they acted as they did.

Slaves

Most of the Greek cities had many slaves who did all types of work. Most slaves had been captured in war.

- A doctor — DR
- A skilled potter — DR
- A dancing girl — DR
- A female house slave — DR
- A mine slave — DR
- A child slave — 70 DR

Write what the slave dealer would have said in selling each of these slaves. How much would he have wanted for each one of them? One is already priced.

© Peter Kent, Sue Cosson and George Middleton. Simon & Schuster Ltd 1993.

7 A Family House

Teacher's notes

Skills

Deducing information from sources
Analysing evidence to assess its usefulness

Attainment targets

Level	AT1a	AT1b	AT1c	AT2	AT3
1					✓
2		✓			✓
3					✓
4					✓
5					✓

Background information

The Greeks used stone for public buildings and it is these which have survived, albeit in ruins. For dwelling houses they used sun-baked mud bricks, sometimes built on stone foundations. Thus we largely know about the form of Greek buildings from foundations that have been excavated. The appearance of the house is largely a matter of conjecture. It is likely that wood was used to make a framework and the roof covered with thatch or clay tiles. The only entrance from the street would be through a narrow doorway leading to a courtyard. This kind of house can still be seen throughout Greece and the Middle East.

Introductory work

Before looking at the sheet, which is about evidence surviving from the past, children could be asked to think about their own houses and what might survive after 2,000 years. What clues might archaeologists of the future find about their lives? The English Heritage book 'Learning from Objects' has excellent ideas for this kind of work.
  Class discussion could focus on these questions:
  How do we know what Greek houses were like?
  How might archaeologists know which room was which?

Using the sheet

Children could compare the house to their own and pick out similarities and differences. Discussion will be needed about the objects. What were they made of and used for? Why did they survive? What kind of family did this house belong to – rich or poor? Children could work in groups to discuss the nature of the objects, compare conclusions and then have access to reference books where they could check their conclusions. They could then cut out the objects, colour them appropriately and write labels.

Extension activities

1 Children could produce a frieze showing life in a Greek house, with the objects being used or worn. This could be done in Greek vase style, using sugar paper (Red on Black or Black on Red).
2 Children could write a story or draw a strip cartoon in which all the objects have to be mentioned in context (e.g. a day in the life of a slave girl or the story of a robber).
3 Children have a list of statements about the Greeks and have to decide whether they are true or false, explaining, with reference to the sheet or other sources, how they decided (e.g. Greek people probably thought it was important to be clean, Greek people probably didn't have Tupperware containers for storing food).
4 Children could discuss how useful these sources are for finding out about Greek home life. What information do they not give? They could be asked to make a list of questions about Greek home life that they would like to ask.

A Family House

Although Greek temples were magnificent, ordinary people's houses in Athens were plain and simple.

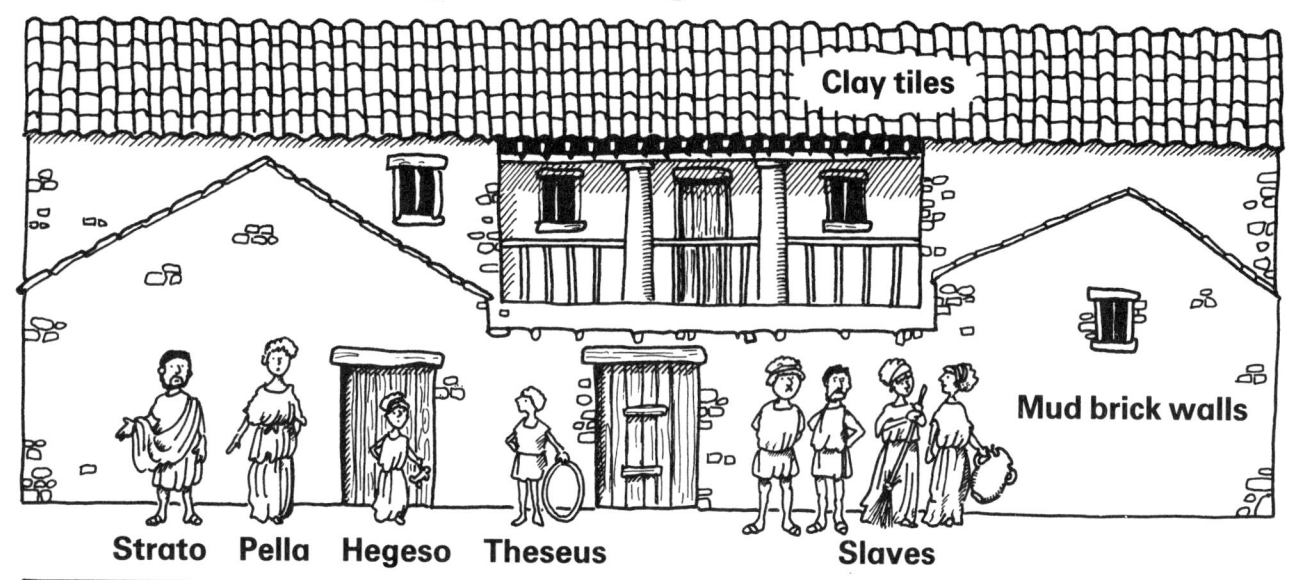

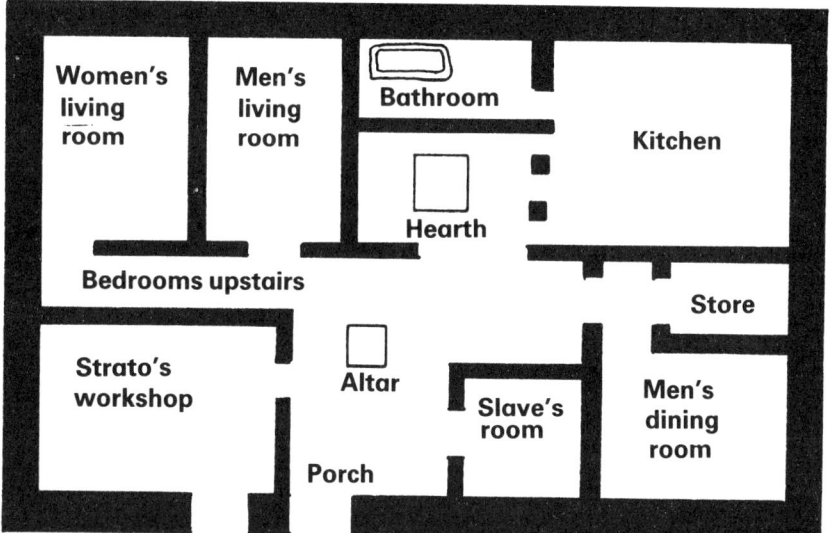

Clay tiles

Mud brick walls

Strato   Pella   Hegeso   Theseus   Slaves

Women's living room | Men's living room | Bathroom | Kitchen | Hearth | Bedrooms upstairs | Store | Strato's workshop | Altar | Slave's room | Men's dining room | Porch

Burglars were known as 'wall diggers', because they simply burrowed through the soft brick walls.

When excavating the ruins of this house, we found these things. Which rooms do you think they belong to?

Make a label for each one saying what you think it is and in which room it was found.

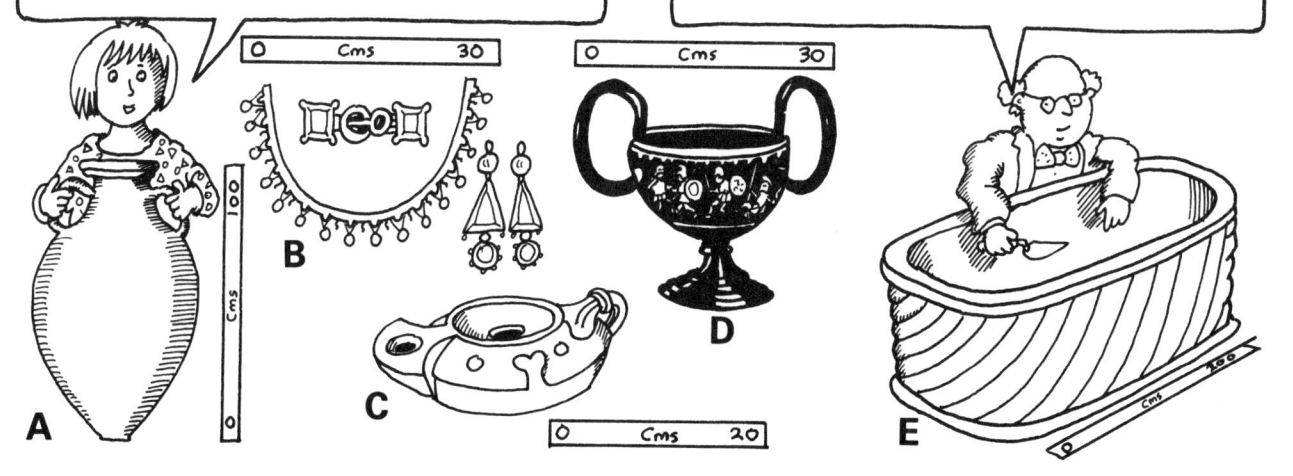

A   B   C   D   E

© Peter Kent, Sue Cosson and George Middleton. Simon & Schuster Ltd 1993.

8 Sea Transport and Trade — Teacher's notes

Skills
Deducing information from a picture source
Putting together information from several sources
Sequencing

Attainment targets

Level	AT1a	AT1b	AT1c	AT2	AT3
1					√
2		√		√	√
3	√			√	√
4				√	√
5					

Background information

As the population of Athens and the other city-states grew, it became necessary to import wheat as there was very little land suited to cereal growing. In addition to wheat, the Greeks imported slaves, metals and dyes. They exported olive-oil, silver, wine, cloth and fine Athenian pottery. Trading with money soon replaced barter.

Ship building and fitting became important industries. Greek merchant ships were less than 30 metres (100 feet) long with a rectangular sail on a single mast. Because of the lack of navigational instruments, sailors tended to follow the shore as much as possible.

Introductory work

Ask children to make and bring in lists of everything at home that has come from another country. (They could be given a check list with particular items to consider, e.g. car, radio, clothes, fruit etc.) Identify these places on a world map and then discuss how the goods came to Britain, why we import these items and what we send to other countries.

Using the sheet

The sheet shows a typical merchant ship being loaded for a voyage around the Eastern Mediterranean. It would be a good idea to discuss the reasons why the Greeks traded and what the items shown suggest about the economy of Athens. Comparisons can be made between the ship shown in the picture and a more modern one. The 'last in, first out' concept of cargo loading activity is sometimes quite difficult for children to understand. It is quite useful to spend some time on this, perhaps with reference to the position of contents in a dustbin. Groups of children could discuss the route they would take if they were captain.

Extension activities

1. After discussion and research about the kind of hazards the ship might meet, children could design a board game that seeks to explain factors that help or hinder a successful voyage.
2. Children could be asked to read this description of a wreck and in groups try to work out:
   a) where it was going   c) what was the reason for the voyage
   b) where it was from   d) what happened to it.

   This small ship was found not far from the island of Rhodes. It has a large hold in which were found 250 amphorae containing wine and almonds. The ship was found in deep water and the timbers were scattered over a wide area. Parts of the ship still haven't been found.

   Different groups can compare their accounts and discuss the reasons for differing interpretations.

Sea Transport and Trade

The sea was a very important trade route for the Greeks. Many of them lived in colonies outside Greece. Even within Greece, it was easier to send goods by sea rather than by bad roads over the mountains. Greek merchant ships were small and tubby. They were propelled mainly by sails, not oars.

The Greeks used these for anchors.

Map locations: Pireaus, Skyros, Lesbos, Celenderis, Greece, You are here, Corinth, Delos, Thera, Rhodes, Kos, Salamis, Dorus, Alexandria, Africa, Egypt

Cargo labels: Grain (Delos), Dates, Spices (Celenderis, Kos), Wine (Thera, Corinth), Olive Oil, Rhodes, Lesbos, Dorus, Alexandria, Skyros, Salamis

The ship is going to Alexandria, calling at the other ports on the way. Choose your route, and load the cargo into the ship in the right order. Copy out a list for the captain.

© Peter Kent, Sue Cosson and George Middleton. Simon & Schuster Ltd 1993.

9 Farming

Teacher's notes

Skills

Sequencing
Using reference books

Attainment targets

Level	AT1a	AT1b	AT1c	AT2	AT3
1					
2	✓		✓		
3	✓				
4	✓				
5					

Background information

Ancient Greek farming was often little more than peasant subsistence farming, although some parts of the country were more fertile and could produce abundance in some years. As well as the growing of grapes, olives and grain mentioned on the sheet, sheep and goats were kept, as they are in modern Greece. Oxen were used as draft animals. It is important to remember that the city-states were supported almost entirely by surrounding farms.

Introductory work

It would be good to have some discussion about the problems of working the land and keeping animals without the use of modern machinery. Many children will need to have the importance of olives (for food and oil) explained, since they play a small part in a typical British diet.

Using the sheet

There are two distinct activities here. The first is to look up in the Greek Glossary (Resource Sheet 1) the names of the months, and to sequence them. This is best done by cutting up a photocopy of the sheet, and pasting the pictures on to a larger piece of paper, in the right order, and with space for captions under each. The second activity is to look at the resulting picture of the farming year, and see what is happening during each month. Reference books will help with details of the farmer's work, and captions can be written for the pictures.

Extension activities

1 Although modern machinery was not available to the Greeks, the sheet does show a variety of tools and equipment being used. Children could list these, and find out if modern equivalents are still in use on farms – for example, axes and pruning-knives. It may be possible to set up sequencing exercises by providing (a) photographs of ancient implements, (b) old farm tools from junk shops or sheds, and (c) modern implements.
2 Work on growing crops can lead on to a consideration of food, and the diet of the ancient Greeks. A Greek meal can be planned and eaten in the classroom, with bread (pitta bread is probably the nearest available), grapes, cheese (goat's milk cheese may prove too strong for most children, but there are milder substitutes) and wine (grape juice) to drink. A menu can be designed and decorated, using patterns copied from original sources.
3 The pictures from the sheet could be expanded into a 'through-the-year' frieze for the classroom wall, with pictures copied from vase paintings and other sources.
4 Children could compare the pictures of farming in Ancient Greece with pictures of farming in other periods, e.g. Egyptians, Saxons and 16th century England. They could note the similarities between them and illustrate the continuity on a time-line.

Farming

Not all Greeks lived in cities. Many lived in the countryside. The land was often rocky and hilly, so farming was difficult. The main crops were olives, vines and grain.

Every month the Greek farmer did a different job on the farm. Here is a set of pictures of the months of the year, but they are muddled up. Cut them out and put them in the right order. Write a short description of what the farmer is doing in each picture. Look at the glossary (Resource Sheet 1) and write down the modern English name for each month.

Metageitnion	Maimacterion	Thargelion
Skirophorion	Poseidaion	Boedromion
Munychion	Anthesterion	Gamelion
Pyanopsion	Elaphebolion	Hecatombaion

© Peter Kent, Sue Cosson and George Middleton. Simon & Schuster Ltd 1993.

10 Religion

Teacher's notes

Skills

Deducing information
Identifying similarities and differences

Attainment targets

Level	AT1a	AT1b	AT1c	AT2	AT3
1					
2		✓	✓		
3			✓		✓
4					
5					

Background information

Religion was part of Greek everyday life in a way that may seem strange to us. The gods and goddesses who dwelt on Mount Olympus behaved in many ways like human beings (except that they did not die). They were seen as a family with Zeus at the head. Each god or goddess had a responsibility for a particular aspect of life. Someone whose love life wasn't going well would sacrifice to Aphrodite whereas a health problem might need the help of Asclepius. If their prayers were successful, people would often leave a thank you message to the appropriate god (often in the form of a carving of stone – hence their survival).

Worship took place outside the temple where a sacrifice would be made – a sheep or a bird perhaps – and prayers were said standing, looking towards the sky.

The Greeks were also very superstitious, like other societies of the time, and were influenced by omens – an unusual happening of any kind (compare with our superstitions). Oracles such as the famous one at Delphi were consulted to find out what was going to happen. Unfortunately, the answers were sometimes ambiguous (again, compare with the 'stars'). For example, in 346 BC King Croesus of Sardis was told by the Delphic oracle that if he waged war on the Persians he would destroy a mighty empire. Unfortunately it turned out to be his own!

Introductory work

Children are familiar with the division of responsibility within a school and realise that different people will help with different problems. Discussion could focus on ways of asking for help and perhaps ways of persuading someone who does not seem to be very willing.

Using the sheet

The labelled drawings of the gods and goddesses reveal their particular sphere of influence. The deities and suppliants should be matched, using the clues in the drawing. There are plenty of relevant reference books. The prayers of the characters at the bottom of the sheet could be added as speech balloons.

Extension activities

1. Scenes outside the temple could be acted or mimed.
2. Children could discuss superstitions that are part of modern life and comparisons made with the Ancient Greeks.
3. Children could compose a question to an oracle and a suitably ambiguous answer.
4. Many Greek myths seek to explain natural phenomena, e.g. the story of Persephone. After telling and discussing this story, children could be asked to write and illustrate their own myth to explain a natural phenomenon, e.g. a rainbow, a thunderstorm. If appropriate, these could be compared with Greek stories.

Religion

The Greeks believed there were many gods and goddesses. They were all said to live on Mount Olympus, the highest mountain, where they formed a family. They were worshipped in temples all over Greece, where people brought offerings and asked the gods for advice or help. In some famous temples there were oracles, where a god was thought to speak directly to the priestess. All kinds of people came to ask questions of these oracles.

APHRODITE Goddess of love and beauty

APOLLO God of the sun, music and poetry

ZEUS Ruler of all the Gods

HESTIA Goddess of the home and family

ARES God of War

ARTEMIS Goddess of the moon and hunting. Protector of young girls

ATHENE Goddess of wisdom and war

DEMETER Goddess of plants and farming

PLUTO God of the underworld

POSEIDON God of the sea

Brasidas Phormio Antigone Ammias Phylides Niobe Atalanta

These people have come to ask the Gods for a favour. What do you think they might want and which God would they ask?

© Peter Kent, Sue Cosson and George Middleton. Simon & Schuster Ltd 1993.

11 Language

Teacher's notes

Skills

Recognising similarities and differences

Attainment targets

Level	AT1a	AT1b	AT1c	AT2	AT3
1					
2					
3	√				√
4	√				
5					

Background information

The Greek language has a continuous history of more than 3,000 years and the language spoken in Greece today is directly descended from the ancient language.

Introductory work

Introductory discussion could focus on the significance of a written language and how it makes the transmission of ideas possible. It is useful to divide the class into two halves and read out a list of ingredients or instructions. Allow one half to write down the list and ask the others to commit it to memory. Ask next day for the list!

It is useful to compare the writing of the Greeks with other early civilisations, Egypt, Mesopotamia, China, and ask children to discuss which are most like our writing today.

Using the sheet

The suggestions on the sheet focus on the similarities and differences between the Greek alphabet and our own and on transcribing words. Once children understand that the relationship is between *sounds* rather than actual letters, transcribing is quite straightforward. Children could produce a chart or simply lists of the three different types of letter.

The examples of words to transcribe here have deliberately been confined to Greek names which have entered the English language. With a little help, children might begin to work out the names.

The objects are:

a) a tribute list from the HELLESPONT showing how much was owed by various subject states
b) a bust of DEMOSTHENES
c) a coin from ATHENA (Athens)
d) a vase showing ACHILLES and HECTOR
e) the helmet of MILTIADES
f) the gravestone of PERSEPHONE from THEBES

Extension activities

1. A pairing game could be played where some children have cards with Greek words and others have English words with the same meaning. They have to find their partner and together write a sentence using the English word correctly. A suitable list of words is given on Resource Sheet 2. It is useful to point out that most of these words are concerned with the theatre and music and ask children to deduce what this suggests about the Ancient Greeks.
2. The activity 'Word House' in 'World Studies 8–13' is a game which looks at the contribution of other languages (including Greek) to English. It is lively and great fun!

Language

Greek was the main language of the ancient world. The Greeks were one of the first peoples to create an alphabet of letters, used to form words. Modern Greek uses the same alphabet today. It is because they wrote down their ideas, discoveries and beliefs that we know so much about them. About half the Greeks could read and write.

Here are some examples of Greek writing. Using Resource sheet 2, try to work out what they say.

ἘΛΛΕΣΠΟΝΤΙΟΣ	
ΔΔΔΙΙ	ΑΙΓΙΝΑ
ΗΔΙΙ	ΔΕΛΟΣ
ΔΔΔΔΙΙ	ΛΗΜΝΟΣ
ΗΗΗΗΔΙΙ	ΜΙΛΕΤΥΣ
ΗΗΗΔΔΔΙΙΙΙ	ΡΟΔΟΣ
ΔΔΔΔΔΔΙΙΙΙ	ΘΑΣΟΣ

ΑΧΙΛΕΣ

ΕΧΤΟΡ

ΜΙΛΤΙΑΔΕΣ

ΔΕΜΟΣΘΕΝΕΣ

ΑΘΗΝΑ

ΠΕΡΣΕΦΟΝΙ
ΘΕΒΕΣ

Look at the Greek alphabet on Resource Sheet 2. Which letters look the same and sound the same, which just look the same and which are completely different? Try writing your own name and those of your friends in Greek letters.

© Peter Kent, Sue Cosson and George Middleton. Simon & Schuster Ltd 1993.

12 Myths and Legends

Teacher's notes

Skills

Sequencing a story
Understanding that events can be seen from more than one point of view
Understanding that stories about an event might be different from what really happened

Attainment targets

Level	AT1a	AT1b	AT1c	AT2	AT3
1					✓
2	✓	✓			✓
3					✓
4					✓
5					✓

Background information

Greek myths and legends are wonderful stories and archaeological research has suggested that many of the legends do, in fact, have a historical background. Michael Wood's TV series and book, *In Search of the Trojan War*, set the stories of Homer firmly into history rather than myth. The importance of the Trojan War in Western literature and art cannot be over-emphasised.

Myths of the Minoan civilisation based in Crete may also have historical origins. Excavations at the palace of Knossos have revealed a 'labyrinth', of interconnecting rooms decorated with bull motifs. The word comes from 'labyros', a double-headed axe; the walls in the palace are decorated with this symbol. (Was Daedalus really a consultant architect?)

Using the sheet

The story will be the starting point. It is an old one and was already a favourite with children in classical Athens! It can be read or told to the children, preferably with suitable illustrations with discussion about what happened and the motivation of the people involved. There could be discussion about which parts of the story might have really happened and whether it is intended to have any 'message'. The sheet can be used straightforwardly to write a description of the story in verse or prose, or the pictures could be cut up and children asked to assemble them in the correct order and then write captions.

Extension activities

1. Children could retell the story from the points of view of Daedalus and Icarus as Icarus soars towards the sun.
2. Children could write alternative endings to the story and compare versions.
3. The children could research details of the archaeological excavations at Knossos and discuss which aspects of the Daedalus story might be partially true.
4. This story could be followed by that of Theseus and the Minotaur. Children could draw their own version of the Minotaur, after listening to the story. They could compare their different versions with the illustrations in different books, discuss reasons for the differences and decide whether the interpretations are fact or fiction.
5. Children could write the story (or any other Greek legend with a suitably dramatic incident) as a newspaper reporter might have reported it and use it to produce a newspaper front page with suitable headlines.
6. The stories of the Siege of Troy and of the wanderings of Odysseus lend themselves to all of these approaches.

Myths and Legends

Greek myths and legends, the stories of gods and human heroes, were passed on for centuries by word of mouth. It is because so many were at last written down, however, that these survived to be told today. Most were written in the form of long poems, because that was how people could remember them.

Greek myths tell the stories of the gods and goddesses they believed in. Some legends, like the war against Troy described in Homer's *Iliad*, have their roots in very distant historical events.

1. There, King Minos. I have finished your labyrinth. / Thank you, Daedalus. You are a genius.

2. Stop! The king says you and your son, Icarus, may not leave Crete. / Why? / You know the secret of the labyrinth.

3. How will we ever leave this island? / I've just had an idea.

4. (Daedalus chasing birds)

5. (Daedalus collecting wax from beehive)

6. Will this work, father? / Trust me, son.

7. Beware the sun, son! Fly not too high.

8. Come down!

9. Oh, Icarus! Why didn't you listen?

Above are drawings of the story of Icarus and his father Daedalus. Write the story as a poem. Each picture makes one verse.

© Peter Kent, Sue Cosson and George Middleton. Simon & Schuster Ltd 1993.

13 The Theatre

Teacher's notes

Skills

Comparing ancient with modern – similarities and differences
Reconstructing the past using evidence and imagination.

Attainment targets

Level	AT1a	AT1b	AT1c	AT2	AT3
1				√	
2			√		
3					
4	√				
5					

Background information

Greek theatre stands as a towering achievement, the foundation of all subsequent drama in the western world. It seems to have had its origin in dramatised readings of narrative poems, with different readers taking the parts of the protagonists. The most important of the festivals mentioned on the sheet was held in honour of the god Dionysus, and lasted four days. Women formed part of the audience for tragedies, but the comedies, with their risqué jokes and political satire, were thought unsuitable for them! Music and dance were also important.

Introductory work

The children's main contact with drama will be through television, and some of them may never have seen a live performance of a play. However, drama work in school will have given them an insight into acting a part, and perhaps into the problems of scene and costume changes. Some explanation of the terms 'comedy', 'tragedy' and 'farce' may be needed. However, teachers should be aware that our modern definition of tragedy does not really fit many of the Ancient Greek dramas.

Using the sheet

Introduce the idea of masked drama by reminding the children of the problems of performing in the open air in huge amphitheatres – it is not easy for the audience to see and hear what is going on. Many Ancient Greek theatres were very cleverly built using natural echoes to magnify the sound, for example Epidauros. Children today are used to close-up shots, subtle changes of expression etc., none of which were possible for the Greeks. Characters had to be larger-than-life, and tended not to change over the course of the play. The class can think of characters of their own, and make masks – an activity which can be anything from paper-and-felt-tips to papier maché, clay or other materials.

Extension activities

1. The stories of some of the great Greek plays are not easy to use at KS2, but since many of them are based on myths, this could be an opportunity to introduce the children to some of the classic stories, as re-told in one of the excellent compilations now available. (See Resources.) The class could then take (say) the story of Theseus and the Minotaur, and make their own play, perhaps using masks.
2. Ask the children, working in groups, to prepare a list of things needed for a modern theatre production, e.g. script, lights, costumes, scenery, music etc. Then ask them to go through the list and find out which of these things were used in the Ancient Greek theatre, and what form they took. Reference books will be needed to help. This should help them to see that the basic idea of the theatre has changed little, whereas the details have.

The Theatre

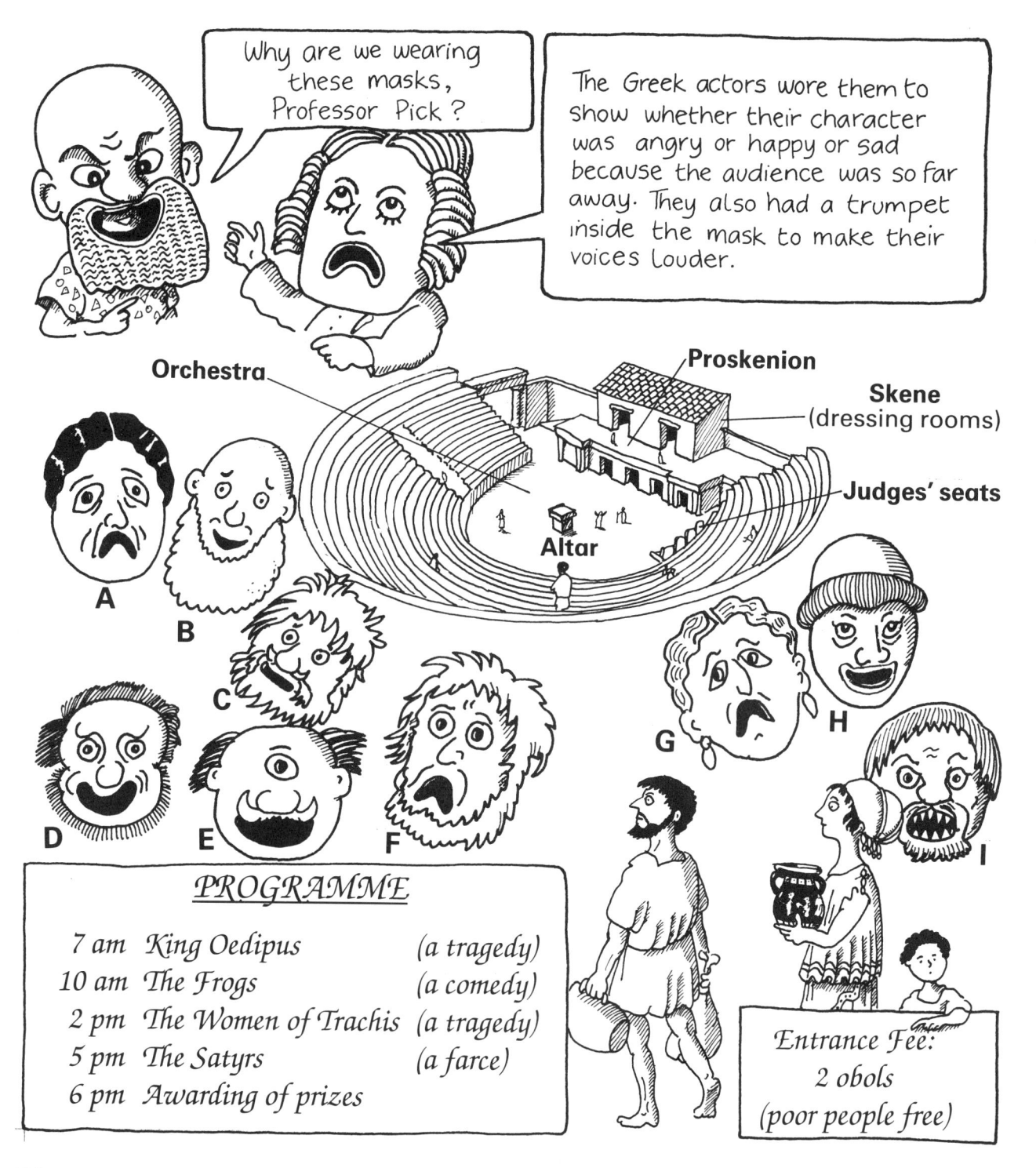

"Why are we wearing these masks, Professor Pick?"

The Greek actors wore them to show whether their character was angry or happy or sad because the audience was so far away. They also had a trumpet inside the mask to make their voices louder.

Orchestra — **Proskenion** — **Skene** (dressing rooms) — **Judges' seats** — **Altar**

A B C D E F G H I

PROGRAMME

7 am	King Oedipus	(a tragedy)
10 am	The Frogs	(a comedy)
2 pm	The Women of Trachis	(a tragedy)
5 pm	The Satyrs	(a farce)
6 pm	Awarding of prizes	

Entrance Fee: 2 obols (poor people free)

Plays were very important to the Greeks. Three or four times a year a festival of plays was held in honour of the gods. The whole city went to watch over several days. The plays were judged and the best given prizes.

Imagine you are getting ready to act in a particular play – either a tragedy, a comedy or a farce. Make or design your own mask to suit your character. Sort out the masks into three groups – one for tragedy, one for comedy and one for farce.

© Peter Kent, Sue Cosson and George Middleton. Simon & Schuster Ltd 1993.

14 Sport

Teacher's notes

Skills
Making comparisons and identifying similarities and differences
Using evidence and identifying its deficiences

Attainment targets

Level	AT1a	AT1b	AT1c	AT2	AT3
1					
2	✓		✓		✓
3	✓				✓
4	✓				✓
5					

Background information

The Greek ideal of 'a healthy mind in a healthy body' lay at the root of their education system. The celebration of physical prowess was bound up with religion (the Olympic Games was originally a religious festival, dedicated to Zeus) and with military training (check how many of the events shown on the sheet are basically military in character). The warring Greek city-states would declare an 'Olympic truce' for three months whilst the Games were on, to allow people to travel to them and participate in safety. The Greeks introduced the ideas of sportsmanship, and competing simply for the glory of winning, although these ideals were not always upheld (some good opportunities for AT2 work here). In some city-states, notably in Sparta, the girls and women took part in sports training and competitions, and there was a parallel event to the Olympics dedicated to Hera, which was restricted to women. However, women could not attend the male Olympics.

Introductory work

Sporting activities span the centuries effortlessly, and the children will need little introduction to the ideas on this sheet. A consideration of the modern Olympic Games will lead to a discussion about the enormous variety of events now held, compared with the ancient Games.

Using the sheet

The main activity here is a comparison of ancient with modern, and identifying similarities and differences. The children could make a chart, listing the events shown on the sheet, with their modern equivalents beside them. A third column could then show ways in which these events have changed, perhaps with small illustrations.

Extension activities

1 Using photographs of original sources, the children could tackle the question 'How do we know about sports in the past?' This could perhaps be approached from the point of view of a modern comparison – what evidence is there for our sports day last year? This can lead on to a consideration of the ancient evidence, and of the inevitable gaps in such evidence.
2 Particularly in an Olympic year (but at other times as well) it can be fun to stage an ancient Olympics. Some concessions to modernity have to be made, but it is possible to involve large numbers of children, not just as athletes but as officials, refreshment sellers, priests and priestesses, heralds etc.
3 Children could investigate changes over time, first by sequencing pictures of (say) an ancient runner, a runner from the 1930s, and a modern athlete: they could then list which things have remained the same about a particular event, and which things have changed.

Sport

Sport was very important to the Greeks. They believed in being fit and healthy. Most young men went to the Gymnasium every day to exercise and meet their friends. Every four years all the top male athletes met at Olympia for the Olympic Games. There were separate games for women.

The Olympic Games were restarted in 1896. Look at the pictures and identify the sports. Do we still have these sports today? If we do, what are the differences? What other events form part of the modern Olympics?

© Peter Kent, Sue Cosson and George Middleton. Simon & Schuster Ltd 1993.

15 Music

Teacher's notes

Skills
Evaluating evidence and its deficiencies
Making deductions

Attainment targets

Level	AT1a	AT1b	AT1c	AT2	AT3
1					
2		✓	✓		✓
3					✓
4				✓	✓
5					

Background information

We know a lot about the importance of music to the Ancient Greeks, but relatively little about the music itself. We know, too, that instrumental music and singing played an integral part in drama and religious ritual, and that music was a vital part of the education of a cultured person. We know, too, that poems such as *The Odyssey* would have been recited to musical accompaniment. Reconstructions of the instruments shown in original sources enable us to hear the *kind* of sounds produced, but the actual music remains a tantalising mystery.

Introductory work

The children could be asked to think about the part played by music in modern life – recreation, ceremonial, religious etc. What materials are musical instruments made of, and how well will they survive? On which occasions might the ancient Greeks have played or listened to music – in other words, why was music important to them?

Using the sheet

A discussion of the different ways of making sound, perhaps using modern equivalents (see below), will lead on to the idea of 'families' of instruments.

Extension activities

1 This sheet provides a good opportunity to consider the partial nature of surviving evidence from the past. The children could be asked to think of other aspects of the Greeks' life about which we can now never know for sure. (For example, the sound of their voices, what they actually thought about, the noise of a busy market, etc.) Tapes are now available of 'music from the ancient world' – if it is possible to obtain one (or better still, two) of these, the children can decide how accurate they are likely to be, and whether one person's version can ever be better than another's.

2 Using modern equivalents of the ancient instruments (bamboo pipes or recorders, plucked string instruments like autoharps, and percussion) the children could create pieces of music to suit different occasions – a happy piece for a wedding, or a slow piece for a sad play.

3 Children could make careful drawings of musicians from vase paintings and sculpture, and build up a frieze of figures playing instruments and singing.

4 From TV and radio, children are familiar with the idea of 'background music'. They could be asked to suggest suitable accompaniment to the speaking of a familiar poem, and perhaps prepare and perform it. A story from *The Odyssey* could be performed in this manner.

5 Can the children devise a simple system for notating the sounds they produce as marks on paper? Can someone else, 'read' their music?

Music

Music was very important to the Greeks. Unfortunately we do not know what theirs sounded like, because they could not record it and we cannot understand the way they wrote music down.

KITHARA　　AULOI　　HARP

A fragment of Greek music

SYRINX　　TIMPANON　　CYMBALS　　LYRE

Draw three columns and label them *blown*, *beaten* and *plucked*. Write the name of each musical instrument in the column you think right for its sound. Do we have anything like them today?

© Peter Kent, Sue Cosson and George Middleton. Simon & Schuster Ltd 1993.

16 Architecture

Teacher's notes

Skills

Gaining information from visual sources
Using reference books

Attainment targets

Level	AT1a	AT1b	AT1c	AT2	AT3
1					√
2		√			√
3		√			√
4					√
5					

Background information

When we think of Ancient Greek architecture, we think of the great stone religious and public buildings. Of course, the houses that most people lived in were simpler in construction (see Sheet 7). There is no doubt, however, that the Greeks established principles of scale, proportion and elegance that have influenced most subsequent western building. The cold, white, 'classical' look of the marble buildings and sculpture today gives a false impression: a riot of colour and gilding seems to have adorned them originally.

Introductory work

The children could be asked to think about the difference between their houses and important public buildings they know, such as churches and office blocks, to introduce the idea of separate styles and materials for different kinds of building. Before seeing photographs or drawings of the great buildings of Ancient Greece, children will need to be reminded that what we have today are *ruins*, they looked very different once.

Using the sheet

The sheet gives a composite picture of a number of key features of Ancient Greek architecture. Using Resource Sheet 3, the children can identify these, and list them, perhaps drawing their own diagrams. (Teachers need to decide for themselves how important it is for the children to learn the technical terms.) Points to be brought out include the technical achievement of raising large buildings in heavy marble, the brilliance of the painted and gilded decoration when they were new, and the number of different craftsmen involved – planners, designers, masons, carpenters, painters, tilers etc. From this information the children can deduce things about the Ancient Greeks – their skill, their motivation, their knowledge of mathematics and geometry, their priorities etc.

Extension activities

1. The design of many public buildings in this country reflects Ancient Greek models. Children could collect postcards and pictures in guide-books of buildings with columns and pediments, etc. (Children must understand that the Ancient Greeks did not build these buildings, but that we are looking at more recent buildings that follow their ideas.)
2. Resource Sheet 4 shows some of the more famous Greek buildings. The children, working in groups, could carry out further research on these, finding out from reference books when they were built, and for what purpose. Using this sheet and Resource Sheet 3, the children could tackle the problem of designing a Greek building.
3. Some children may like to look at the history of one particular site, e.g. the Acropolis in Athens. This could lead to thinking about how we treat our ancient sites, and the value we place on them. The question of the Elgin Marbles from the Parthenon could provide the basis for a class debate.

Architecture

Greek buildings were all built to the same system. Their favourite building material was marble. They used very little mortar or cement. The stone blocks were held together by iron clamps. The statues and carved decorations were painted in bright colours, and sometimes covered in gold.

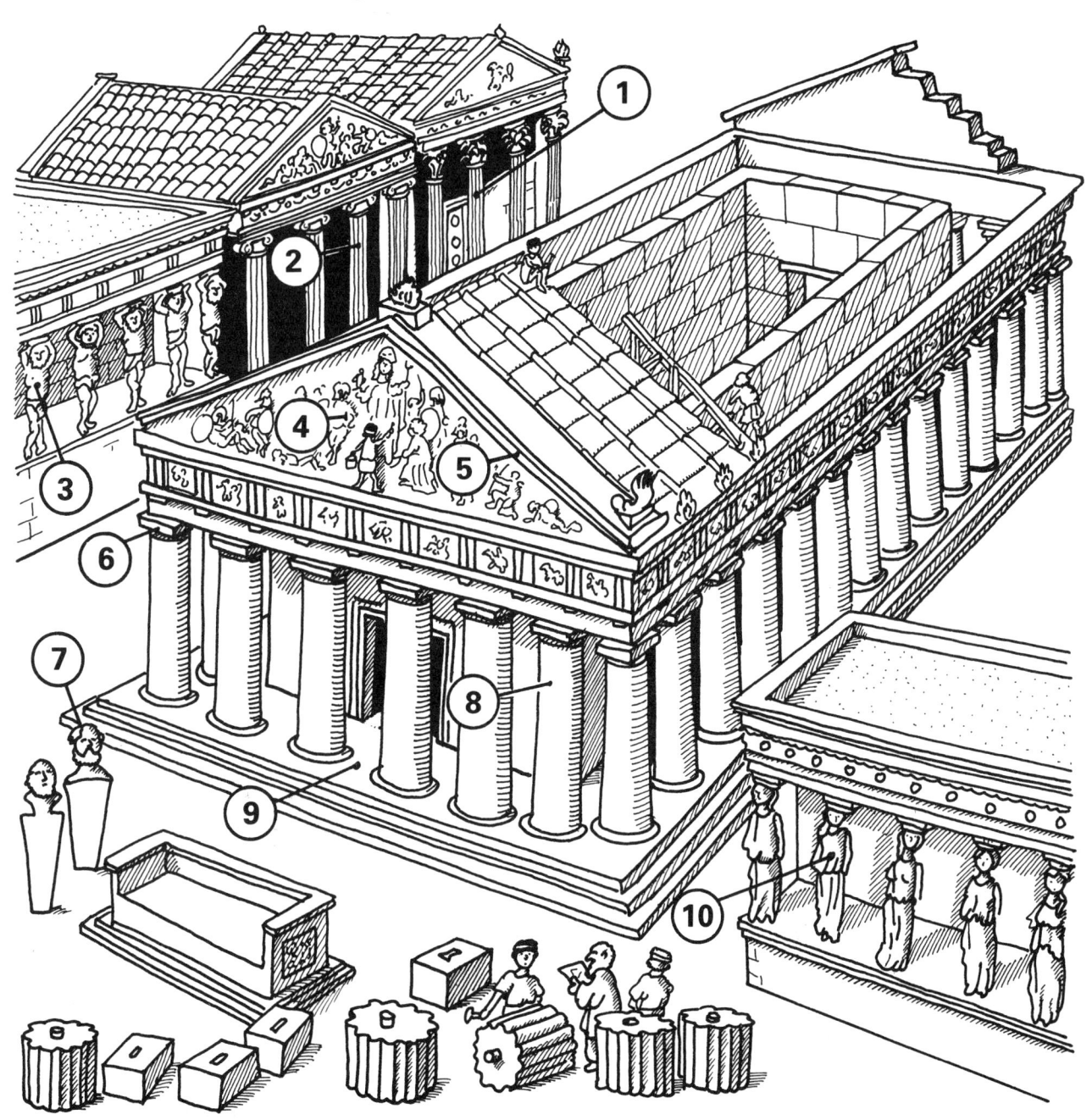

Identify the ten numbered features, using the examples on Resource Sheet 3. Make a key to show the different parts of the building.

You have decided to build a temple. Make a list of all the different types of craftsmen you would need.

© Peter Kent, Sue Cosson and George Middleton. Simon & Schuster Ltd 1993.

17 Sculpture

Teacher's notes

Skills
Sequencing
Reconstructing from incomplete evidence

Attainment targets

Level	AT1a	AT1b	AT1c	AT2	AT3
1					
2					
3	✓				✓
4	✓			✓	
5					

Background information

Greek sculpture was an integral part of their architecture, being used to decorate and support their buildings (see Resource Sheet 3). It was also closely bound up with their religious beliefs – the majority of Greek statues are of gods and goddesses. The Greeks were not so interested in portraying the individual, as in expressing the ideal – hence there are very few portrait statues, and many representations of ideally beautiful men and women. Marble statues have survived better than bronze, which was valuable and often melted down and re-used. A comparison with other cultures of the ancient world reveals the magnitude of the Greeks' achievement – ancient Egyptian statuary, for example, remained formal, static and stylized for over a thousand years, while the Greek style changed over the centuries. It became ever more naturalistic and skilful.

Introductory work

The children may be familiar with statues of local celebrities, and with the idea of commemorating famous people in this way. The idea of religious statues may be introduced by a comparison with a modern Catholic church, where images are used to aid devotion.

Using the sheet

A photocopy of the sheet can be cut up, and the top row of statues rearranged in the correct order, from most stylized to most lifelike. (Since this is a subjective judgement, there may be a chance here for some variation in opinion, supported by argument!) The statues could be coloured, since it seems certain that originally marble statues, at least, were painted. The bottom row of illustrations can be reconstructed, and the missing parts drawn in, perhaps reference books to find similar sculptures for guidance. The point should be made that no one can know for certain what the missing pieces were like.

Extension activities

1. Many teachers will want to experiment with craft activities on this theme. Clay can be modelled to produce 'statues' of characters from Greek myths, although anything over about 25 cm high will need a wire armature for support. Clay figures can be modelled in low relief on a flat slab.
2. A collection could be made of drawings and/or photographs of statues to be found locally, either free-standing or as part of buildings. This could lead to a discussion about why statues are made – e.g. to commemorate a famous person, to inspire worship, to remember an event (war memorial) and so on.
3. Sheet 10 (Religion) could be used in conjunction with this one, to identify the various gods and goddesses portrayed in sculpture, and to discover details about their attributes and associated legends.

Sculpture

The Greeks were the first people to make lifelike statues of people. Some were made of marble and some of bronze. Over the years, sculpture became more and more lifelike. Put these statues in the order you think they were made, the oldest first.

A   **B**   **C**   **D**   **E**

A STATUE FROM THE TEMPLE OF ZEUS

A STATUE OF APHRODITE

A STATUE OF VICTORY

Most statues that remain today are broken. Draw how you think the missing parts would have been sculpted. Compare your drawing with your friends'. If they are different, can you see why?

© Peter Kent, Sue Cosson and George Middleton. Simon & Schuster Ltd 1993.

18 Scientists and Philosophers — Teacher's notes

Skills

Using reference books
Debating

Attainment targets

Level	AT1a	AT1b	AT1c	AT2	AT3
1				✓	✓
2					✓
3					
4					
5					

Background information

Plato (*c.* 427–*c.* 347 BC) was a pupil of Socrates, and one of the greatest philosophers of all time. His ideas about the meaning of life, and of how a state should be governed, still influence thinkers today.

Aristotle (384–322 BC) was a pupil of Plato, and became the teacher of Alexander the Great. He wrote many books embracing and classifying virtually everything that was then known about the world.

Archimedes (*c.* 287–212 BC) worked on many scientific problems, and is best known for formulating the principle about the apparent loss in weight of an object in a liquid.

Euclid (active about 300 BC) was the first person to set down systematically the principles of geometry.

Pythagoros (582–*c.* 507 BC) was a philosopher as well as a mathematician, and taught about the way to purify the soul. He is best known for the theorem in geometry that bears his name.

Hippocrates (*c.* 460–*c.* 377 BC) 'The Father of Medicine', brought to healing a scientific approach based on observation and common sense.

Introductory work

This is not an easy sheet to use with young children, but the ideas involved are important. Begin by mentioning famous scientists and inventors of more modern times – the children may have come across the names of Einstein, Alexander Fleming, Marie Curie, John Logie Baird etc.

Bring out the point that sometimes one person gets an idea which then influences almost everyone else, and starts other people thinking too.

Using the sheet

The class could split into six groups, with each group being given one of the people on the sheet to research, using reference books in the classroom or library. Then a debate could take place, with each group being given the chance to make a presentation in favour of their person for the honour of the statue. Discussion could be encouraged about whether machines are more important than medicine, or whether trying to find meaning in the world is more important than anything else.

Extension activities

1 The children could mark the lives of these people on a time-line, which will raise the problem of the lack of precision in some of the dates. A discussion could follow about why we may not know exactly when someone in the past was born or died, and this could be compared with the highly documented society in which we live now.

2 From their work on Sheet 4 (Growing Up) the children could start to answer the question, 'Why are there no women on this sheet?'

Scientists and Philosophers

Greek scientists and philosophers tried to work out why the world is the way it is, and why we do the things we do. Their work influenced later thinkers and was the foundation of our modern world.

PLATO
PHILOSOPHER
Wrote a book saying what the ideal government should be.

ARISTOTLE
PHILOSOPHER & SCIENTIST
He divided what we know into subjects

SCIENCE ART THEOLOGY

ARCHIMEDES
INVENTOR
He invented machines and discovered the power of the lever

EUCLID
MATHEMATICIAN
Worked out the principles of geometry

PYTHAGOROS
MATHEMATICIAN
Made great discoveries in mathematics

πr^2

HIPPOCRATES
DOCTOR
He taught that disease was not caused by the anger of the Gods

Your school is to put up a statue to one of these famous thinkers. Which one do you think it should be?

© Peter Kent, Sue Cosson and George Middleton. Simon & Schuster Ltd 1993.

19 The Persian Wars

Teacher's notes

Skills

Assigning reasons for historical events
Researching in reference books

Attainment targets

Level	AT1a	AT1b	AT1c	AT2	AT3
1					
2		✓			
3		✓			
4		✓			
5		(✓)			

Background information

In most city-states of Ancient Greece all young men were expected to serve in the army. In Sparta, in particular, the men spent most of their lives under military discipline. As a result, Greece could call on a force of well-trained and equipped soldiers to defend the country from invaders.

Introductory work

This sheet gives a good opportunity to discuss why things happen. This can be done by imagining an apparently trivial modern example, e.g. 'Why did Alan fight Colin in the playground today? Because he took his pencil-sharpener.
   "Ah, but, yesterday Alan hid one of Colin's trainers after games. And the two of them have never really been friends since Alan got picked for the school team and Colin didn't. Mind you, the families don't get on very well – wasn't there that incident with the dog? And I know Colin's not feeling too good today – I think he's worried about his Mum . . ." A discussion like this can point out the difficulty of being clear and confident about the reasons for anything.

Using the sheet

The sheet summarises the events of the wars, and Resource Sheet 5 gives more details about sea warfare. The children could compare the two soldiers on the sheet, and discuss their relative strengths and weaknesses.

Extension activities

1 The story of the battle of Marathon, and the epic run of Pheidippedes, would make a good subject for a series of illustrations and captions, strip cartoon style, telling the story along the classroom wall.
2 To tackle the question of 'The Reason Why', the children could be supplied with cards giving a number of reasons for the Persian invasions of Greece. Some of these will be absurd, and some possible. The children discuss them, and sort them out. They will be left with a number of possible reasons, all of which could have some foundation. (Examples: The Persians invaded because they wanted revenge on the Greeks. The Persians invaded because they were jealous of Greek sea power. The Persians invaded because they were very fond of olives.)
3 Children could research into the modern Marathon race, now run by so many – though without taking part in a desperate battle first! When was it first run? What is the world record time for men and women? What are the names of famous Marathon runners? A group could report to the whole class on their findings.
4 Some of the class could role-play a group of women left in Athens while the battle goes on. They discuss the rights and wrongs of the conflict, share their fears and hopes, and discuss what they will do if the Greek army loses.

The Persian Wars

The Greeks were threatened by their powerful eastern neighbour, the Persian Empire. In 490 BC the King of Persia, Darius, led a gigantic army into Greece. An estimated 100,000 Persians met 11,000 Greeks on the plain of Marathon. There was a great and fierce battle. Amazingly, the Greeks won.

Most of the Greeks were heavily armed and were called *hoplites*.

- Horsehair crest
- Bronze helmet
- Cuirass of bronze or leather
- Spear
- Bronze shield
- Short sword
- Bronze greaves
- A Greek soldier

MARATHON

The athlete Pheidippides ran to Athens with news of the victory.

42.186 km

We've won!

Then he died.

The Persian army contained archers, spearmen and cavalry.

- A Persian soldier
- Padded jacket
- Spear
- Quiver of arrows
- Bow

Ten years later the Persians came back to Greece. This time they captured Athens and burnt it down. Fortunately for the Greeks they beat the Persians the same year in a great sea battle at Salamis. (See Resource Sheet 5).

You are a spy working for Darius. Write a report for him pointing out the strengths and weaknesses of the Greek army.

© Peter Kent, Sue Cosson and George Middleton. Simon & Schuster Ltd 1993.

20 Greece and Rome

Teacher's notes

Skills

Identifying similarities and differences
Relating different aspects of a historical situation

Attainment targets

Level	AT1a	AT1b	AT1c	AT2	AT3
1					
2					
3			✓		
4			✓		
5			✓		

Background information

In 146 BC, Greece became a Roman province. Usually a conquering nation imposes its ideas on the conquered, but in this case, when the Romans conquered Greece, they absorbed much of Greek culture.

Large numbers of Greek slaves were taken to Rome and were highly prized as doctors and teachers. Many well-born young Romans had Greek tutors and often completed their education in Athens.

The Romans also adopted many Greek ideas about art and architecture. There are many similarities between Greek and Roman religious belief.

Introductory work

It would be useful to discuss how we are influenced by ideas from other people (pizzas and Big Macs might be a useful starting point) and how we often copy people we admire (brands of clothes worn by sports stars are quite a good example). The class could perhaps consider which nations influence lifestyles in Britain today.

Using the sheet

The illustrations are intended to show composite pictures of Greek and Roman cities in order to highlight ways in which the Romans were influenced by the Greeks.

This could be approached by looking at the Greek city and asking children to find evidence of different amenities – places for buying and selling, worship, entertainment, medical help, etc. They could then look at the Roman city and decide whether it had the same amenities. Is there anything lacking or anything extra?

Close observation will then be needed to decide whether each activity or building is:
   a) exactly the same (e.g. selling slaves)
   b) the same in some respects (e.g. the temple – same structure but different columns)
   c) quite different (e.g. the theatre construction)

After explaining to the children that Greece was conquered by the Romans, discussion could focus on whether there is any evidence to suggest that Greek ideas spread to Rome.

Extension activities

1   A more difficult activity would be to discuss the features of the Greek city and then give the children the picture of the Roman city and ask them to try to work out which one came first and identify who had copied from whom.
2   Children could be asked to imagine that they are a young Greek who has been sent to Rome to be sold as a slave. Another slave asks him or her what their home city is like and in what ways it is like or unlike Rome. Write or make a tape recording of the description.

Greece and Rome

In about 150 BC the Romans conquered Greece and made it part of their empire. Greek colonial cities in Italy and Sicily had first brought Greek ideas to the west. The Romans admired and borrowed many of them.

A GREEK CITY

A ROMAN CITY

Look at the pictures of the two cities. How many things appear to be the same? How many are different?

© Peter Kent, Sue Cosson and George Middleton. Simon & Schuster Ltd 1993.

Resource Sheet 1

Greek Glossary

Acropolis	A fortress on a hill within a Greek city
Agora	An open market and meeting place
Amphora	A large pot with two handles for storing liquids
Anthesterion	The second month of the year
Boedromion	The ninth month of the year
Caryatid	A supporting column carved in the shape of a woman
Chiton	A linen tunic worn by men and women
Drachma	The main Greek coin
Ephor	One of the five leaders of Sparta
Elaphebolion	The third month of the year
Gamelion	The first month of the year
Gymnasium	A place where athletes trained
Hecatombaion	The seventh month of the year
Helot	A slave of the Spartans
Himation	A cloak worn by men and women
Hoplite	A heavily armed foot soldier
Maimacterion	The eleventh month of the year
Metageitnion	The eighth month of the year
Munychion	The fourth month of the year
Obol	A sixth of a drachma
Orchestra	The round space of beaten earth at the centre of the theatre
Polis	A Greek city state
Poseidaion	The twelfth month of the year
Proskenion	The raised stage in the theatre
Pyanopsion	The tenth month of the year
Skene	The dressing rooms in the theatre
Skirophorion	The sixth month of the year
Stoa	A long, covered passageway with columns
Strategos	One of the ten generals of Athens
Trireme	A warship with three rows of oars
Trierarch	The captain of a trireme
Thargelion	The fifth month of the year
Tholos	A domed building used as a council chamber

© Peter Kent, Sue Cosson and George Middleton. Simon & Schuster Ltd 1993.

Resource Sheet 2

The Greek Alphabet

	Name	Sound			Name	Sound
Α	alpha	a		Ν	nu ('ni')	n
Β	vita	v		Ξ	xi	x (ks)
Γ	gamma	gh (or 'y' before 'i' or 'e' sounds)		Ο	omikron	o (as in 'got')
Δ	delta	dh		Π	pi	p
Ε	epsilon	e		Ρ	rho	r
Ζ	zita	z		Σ	sigma	s
Η	ita	i		Τ	tau ('taf')	t
Θ	thita	th		Υ	ipsilon	i, y
Ι	iota	i		Φ	phi	ph
Κ	kapa	k		Χ	khi	kh
Λ	lambda	l		Ψ	psi	ps
Μ	mu ('mi')	m		Ω	omega	o (as in 'home')

Numbers

Ι	= 1		Η	=	100
Π	= 5		Χ	=	1,000
Δ	= 10		Μ	=	10,000

Greek origins of some English words

Greek	English	Greek	English
ΑΛΦΑΒΗΤΑ	alphabet	ΑΡΑΧΝΟΦΟΒΙΑ	arachnophobia
ΙΔΕΑ	idea	ΧΟΡΟΣ	chorus
ΚΡΙΣΙΣ	crisis	ΣΥΜΦΩΝΙΑ	symphony
ΘΕΑΤΡΟ	theatre	ΚΑΤΑΣΤΡΟΦΗ	catastrophe
ΠΕΡΙΠΑΤΟΣ	peripatetic	ΠΑΡΕΝΘΕΣΙΣ	parenthesis
ΒΙΒΛΙΟ	book	ΠΡΩΛΟΓΟΣ	prologue
ΟΡΧΕΣΤΡΑ	orchestra	ΦΙΛΟΣΟΦΟΣ	philosopher
ΦΟΒΙΑ	phobia	ΥΠΟΚΡΙΤΟΣ	hypocrite

© Peter Kent, Sue Cosson and George Middleton. Simon & Schuster Ltd 1993.

Resource Sheet 3

Greek Architecture

Greek column design was based on three types: the **Doric** (c. 600 BC), the **Ionic** (c. 500 BC) and the **Corinthian** (c. 450 BC).

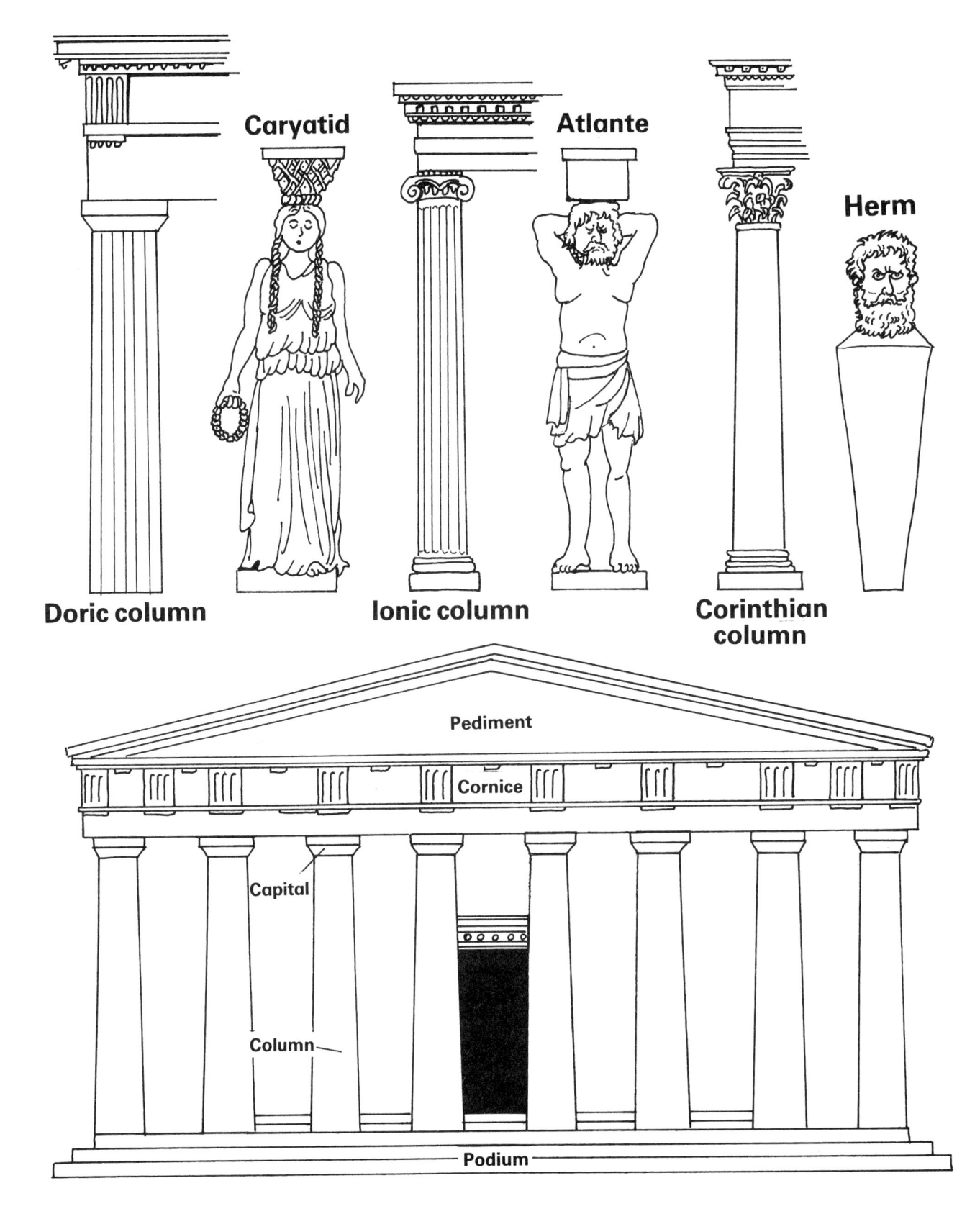

Doric column — Caryatid — **Ionic column** — Atlante — **Corinthian column** — Herm

Pediment — Cornice — Capital — Column — Podium

© Peter Kent, Sue Cosson and George Middleton. Simon & Schuster Ltd 1993.

Resource Sheet 4

Famous Greek Buildings

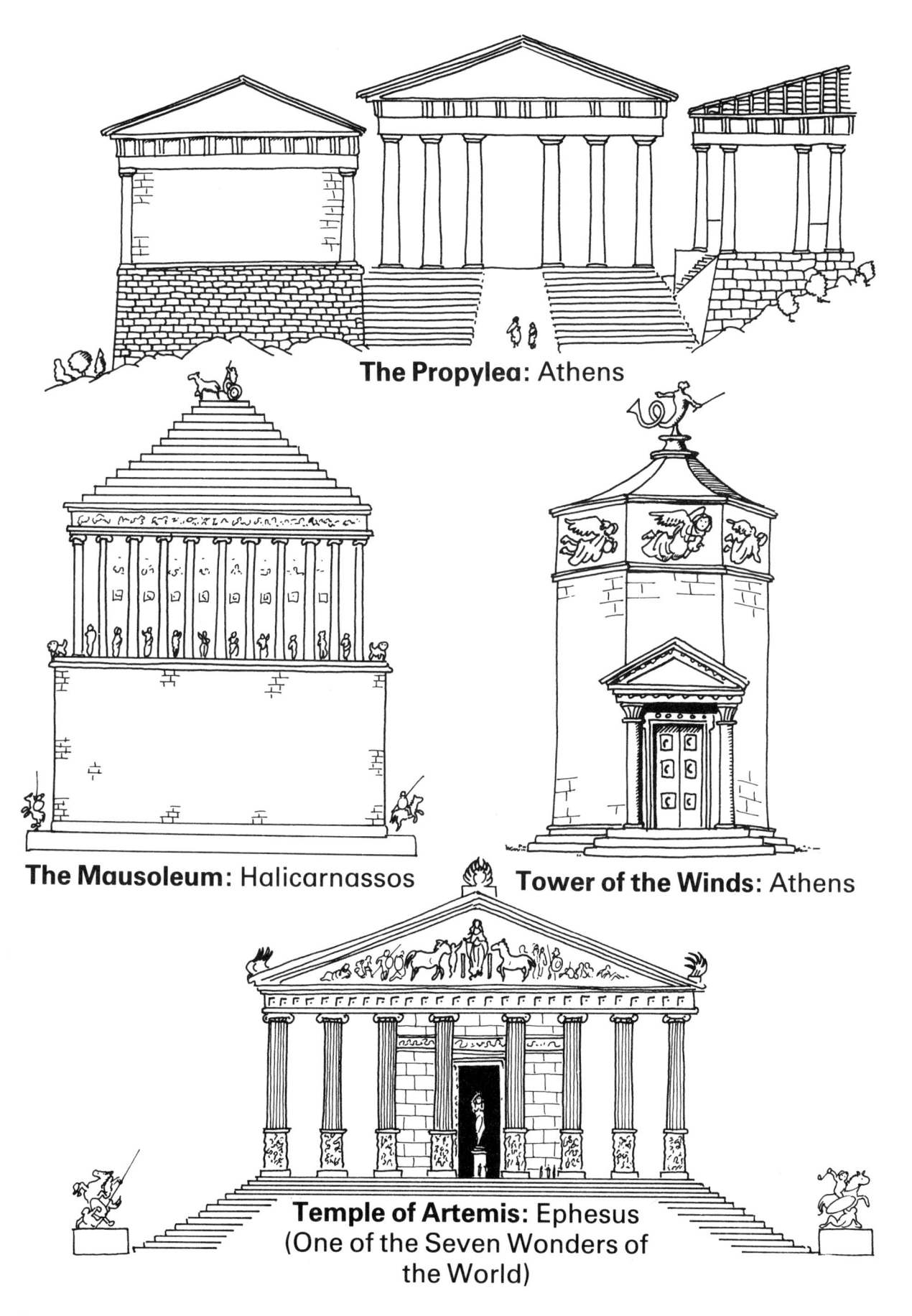

The Propylea: Athens

The Mausoleum: Halicarnassos

Tower of the Winds: Athens

Temple of Artemis: Ephesus
(One of the Seven Wonders of the World)

© Peter Kent, Sue Cosson and George Middleton. Simon & Schuster Ltd 1993.

Resource Sheet 5

A Greek Trireme

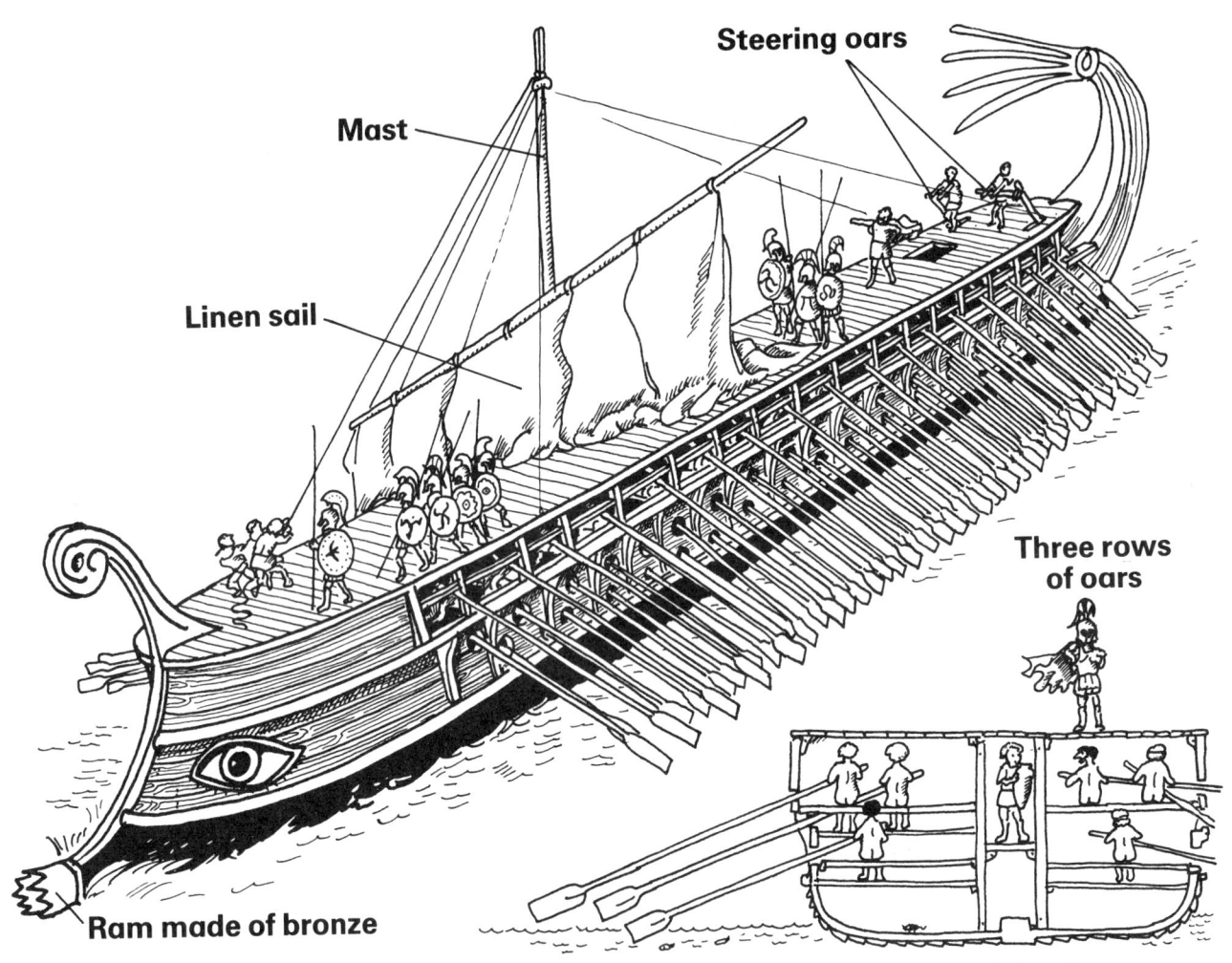

Labels on diagram: Steering oars, Mast, Linen sail, Three rows of oars, Ram made of bronze

A typical trireme was about 35 metres long and 5 metres wide. It had a crew of 170 rowers (these were *not* slaves), ten officers, sixteen soldiers and a captain called a *trierarch*.

Over short distances a speed of sixteen kilometres per hour could be reached.

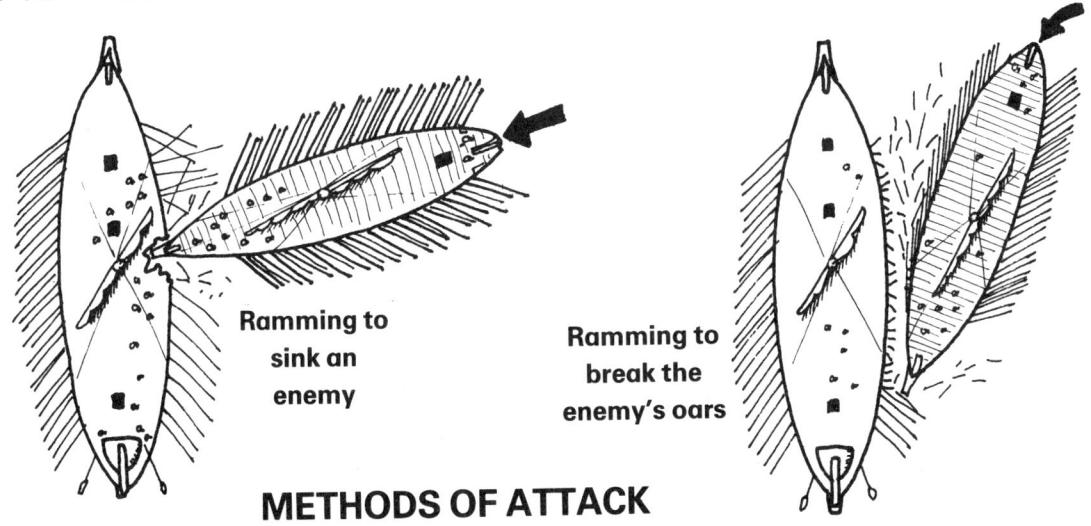

Ramming to sink an enemy

Ramming to break the enemy's oars

METHODS OF ATTACK

© Peter Kent, Sue Cosson and George Middleton. Simon & Schuster Ltd 1993.

Resource Sheet 6

Greek Costume

Greek clothes were very simple. They were usually made of wool or linen. A large piece of cloth was called a *chiton*. This was draped and fastened with pins or brooches. Young men and slaves wore short chitons; women and old men wore long ones.

Chiton

Hats

Himation

Chiton

Boot

Sandal

Himation

© Peter Kent, Sue Cosson and George Middleton. Simon & Schuster Ltd 1993.

Resource Sheet 7

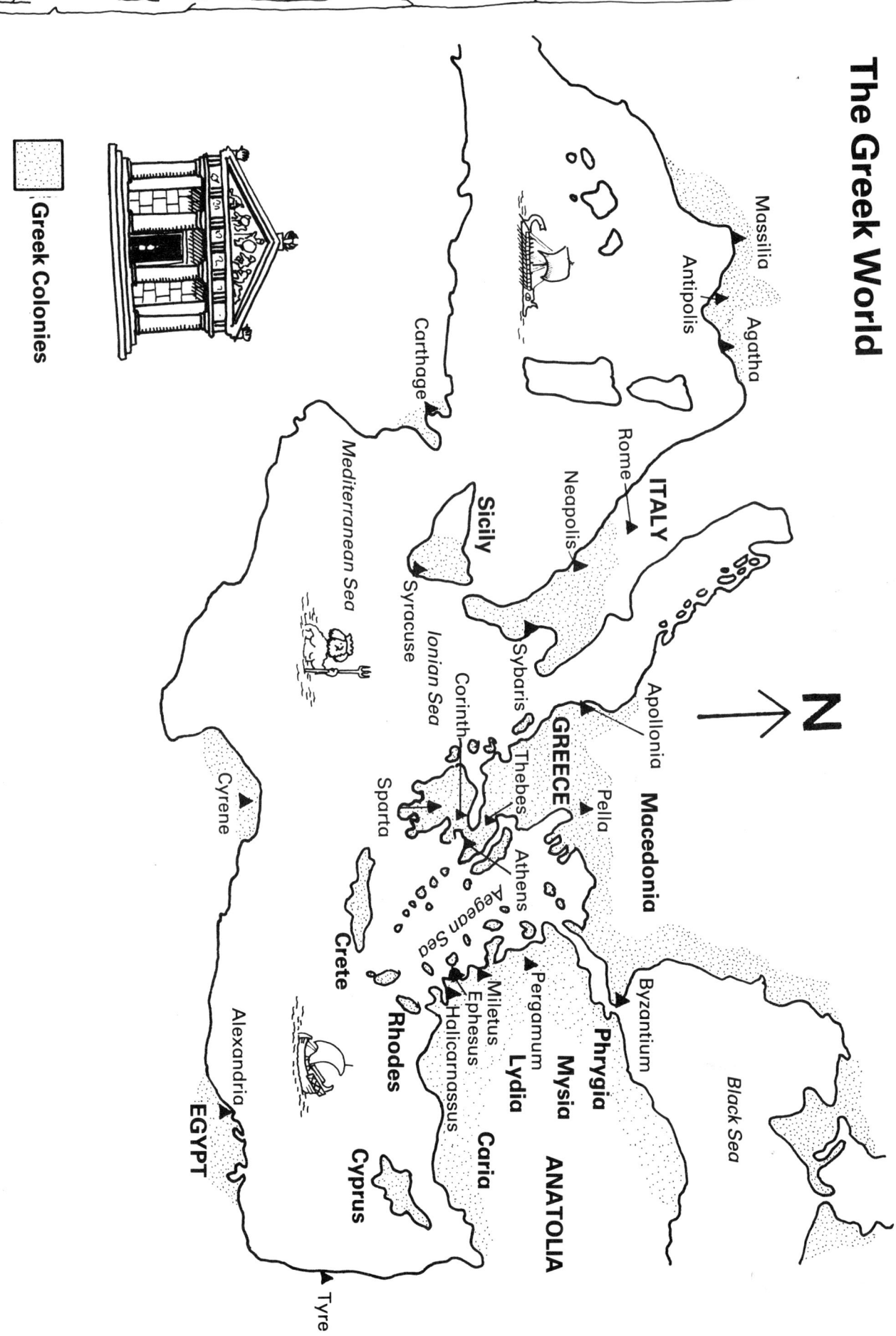

The Greek World

Greek Colonies

Places labeled on map:
- Massilia
- Antipolis
- Agatha
- Carthage
- Rome
- ITALY
- Neapolis
- Sicily
- Syracuse
- Sybaris
- Mediterranean Sea
- Ionian Sea
- Corinth
- Apollonia
- Macedonia
- Pella
- Thebes
- GREECE
- Sparta
- Athens
- Aegean Sea
- Byzantium
- Black Sea
- Crete
- Rhodes
- Miletus
- Ephesus
- Halicarnassus
- Pergamum
- Phrygia
- Mysia
- Lydia
- Caria
- ANATOLIA
- Cyprus
- Cyrene
- Alexandria
- EGYPT
- Tyre

N →

© Peter Kent, Sue Cosson and George Middleton. Simon & Schuster Ltd 1993.